IMAGES
of America

THE FLEISCHMANN YEAST FAMILY

Charles Fleischmann, a Jewish immigrant from Silesia, became a confidant of presidents, a Kentucky colonel, and one of the richest men in America.

IMAGES
of America

THE FLEISCHMANN YEAST FAMILY

P. Christiaan Klieger

ARCADIA

Copyright ©2004 by P. Christiaan Klieger
ISBN 0-7385-3341-6

Published by Arcadia Publishing
Charleston SC, Chicago, Portsmouth NH, San Francisco

Printed in Great Britain

Library of Congress Catalog Card Number: 2004111532

For all general information contact Arcadia Publishing at:
Telephone 843-853-2070
Fax 843-853-0044
E-mail sales@arcadiapublishing.com
For customer service and orders:
Toll-Free 1-888-313-2665

Visit us on the internet at http://www.arcadiapublishing.com

to Ann, Bruce, and Christian

CONTENTS

FOREWORD

Dr. P. Christiaan Klieger's book, Images of America – the Fleischmann Yeast Family, recounts the life of Charles Fleischmann, my great, great grandfather, his brothers Louis and Max, as well as the lives of many of Charles' often colorful and successful descendents.

Dr. Klieger has thoroughly researched and captured the lives of the Fleischmanns within my branch of the family. These include my great grandmother, Bettie Fleischmann Holmes, her husband, Dr. Christian Rasmus Holmes, and their three sons, Carl Fleischmann Holmes, Christian Rasmus Holmes II, and Julius Fleischmann Holmes.

We are all shaped by stories, and this book is full of interesting tales and images. Growing up, I was particularly influenced by family recollections of the lives of Charles Fleischmann and his son-in-law, Dr. Christian Holmes. These were first-generation immigrants, respectively from Austria-Hungary and Denmark, who made a great difference in the lives of others. Dr. Christian Holmes combined his engineering and scientific skills to establish in Cincinnati one of the leading hospitals in America; his wife, Bettie Fleischmann Holmes, and her brother, Julius Fleischmann, supported his efforts politically and financially. Like his father-in-law, Charles, Dr. Holmes was a serious man, focused on work and his family.

Charles built the present-day equivalent of an industrial, biotech empire, passing on significant wealth to his children. His daughter, Bettie, aggressively led efforts to repeal Prohibition, and was a major benefactor of the arts in Cincinnati and New York City. She amassed a significant collection of Chinese art. Charles' son, Maximillian, created the Max Fleischmann Foundation, which sustained critical research in science and education. Charles' eldest son, Julius, continued to build the Fleischmann Company into a major industrial complex, and several of his descendents have had a lasting effect on education and the arts. My great uncles, his nephews, told me that Julius was a highly respected businessman, a wise, generous man, as well as a first-rate athlete.

This book recounts in some detail the lives of many of the descendents of Charles Fleischmann, including that of Charles Fleischmann's grandson, Christian Holmes II, my grandfather. Here was a man who worked and played hard. A highly decorated World War I veteran, he acquired, significantly landscaped, and expanded Coconut Island in Hawai`i. He built up a major fishing business, owned two large private zoos in Hawai`i and California, and enjoyed a significant collection of rare orchids, books and Asian art. Interestingly, his island, the base for his commercial fishing operations and collection of marine life, has subsequently become the site of one of the most important marine biology research stations in the country.

There are really two stories about the Fleischmanns. One story is about what the Fleischmanns did: how immigrant brothers in one generation built a major industrial enterprise, made lasting contributions to their communities and passed on significant wealth to their descendents, many of whom led highly successful lives. The second story is about what the Fleischmanns were "like." I see this reappearing drive to live large lives, sustained by unusual energy and creativity. In this pursuit of a large life, there have been spectacular successes and failures, and the human toll has been significant.

I have personally known members of four generations of Fleischmanns, and I like being around them. I find them on balance to be creative, artistic, eccentric, funny, driven and restless. I have found some to possess an unusual elegance and intelligence, many of them to be quite caring. They tend to do, as this book demonstrates, very interesting things.

Christian R. Holmes IV

Photo & Art Credits

A—Author's collection. Advertising courtesy of Fleischmann Yeast Division of Burns, Philp-North America.
AH—Ann Holmes Terrell collection.
AP—Associated Press, Oakland Museum of California Oakland Tribune Collection.
B—Bruce Spaulding collection.
BP—Burns, Philp
BPBM—Bishop Museum.
C—Cincinnati Museum Center.
CL—Public Library of Cincinnati and Hamilton County
CF—Charles Fleischmann III collection.
CH—Christian Holmes IV collection.
F—Martin Fischer.
FH—Frank Harata collection.
GN—Gary Nakamoto.
HF—Hillforest Historic Site.
HIMB—Hawai`i Institute of Marine Biology.
LZ—Lester Zukeran.
M—Mystic Seaport Museum.
N—University of Nevada-Reno, Special Collections.
P—Peekskill City Library.
PF—Edwin W. Pauley Collection, UCLA Special Collections.
S—Skene Memorial Library, Fleischmanns, New York.
SB—Santa Barbara Museum of Natural History
TB—Tom Beyer.
TL—Truman Library.
U—U.S. Patent Office.
USAF—United States Air Force.

INTRODUCTION

Imagine the commercial snap of a simple, natural product that reproduces itself a thousand times in a few hours, utilizing only the most basic of ingredients. While fermentation has been known by humanity for thousands of years, this book is a story of a talented family who harnessed the full potential of the tiny yeast microbe—a wildly successful enterprise whose goal was the provision of some of the good things in life to the broadest possible market. Yeast not only made bread rise, it produced alcohol, and with a few juniper berries, became gin. With the aid of another microbe, a bacterium, some of the alcohol was consumed to produce vinegar, which was an essential ingredient in products from dill pickles to ammunitions. Totally contrary to the specter of bioterrorism that microbial husbandry heralds today, the Fleischmann yeast and distilling companies brought only thoughts of warm, freshly baked bread and ice cold martinis.

Other than two brief corporate histories (at the 50th and 125th anniversaries), the Fleischmann story has not been told. Nor has much been written about the generations of outrageously successful Fleischmanns for whom societal progress, openhearted philanthropy, and exotic adventure were hard wired.

I discovered the Fleischmann family in a rather backwards manner—back at my old curator job at Bishop Museum in Honolulu, I was asked to write a local history of a tiny, 21-acre islet in Kane`ohe Bay, O`ahu. Originally a volcanic dike in the center of the now-sunken Ko`olau caldera, Coconut Island was radically terraformed in the 1930s into a perfect island retreat for one of the more flamboyant heirs of the Fleischmann yeast family, Christian R. Holmes II. But digging into the background of Mr. Holmes, I discovered the tremendous accomplishments of his mother Bettie, and his uncles Max and Julius Fleischmann. That brought me back to the truly original genius of the family, Charles (Carl), the founder of the company. What was consistent through 135 years of Fleischmanns in America is a remarkable history of achievement: well-timed business acumen, political dexterity, and the cultivation of civilization.

The Fleischmann story also reveals landmark innovations in the history of American advertising, with perhaps the first and most successful application of the brand name concept that was to dominate the American market to this day. Founded in 1868 by Charles and Maximillian Fleischmann, recent immigrants from the Austrian Empire, Fleischmann Yeast found a market in the great post-Civil War expansion of rural settlers moving westward. Home baking was the rule of the day, and the brothers' product was far superior to the rather haphazard leavening agents then being used. Utilizing a superb distribution network (another innovation), sales and profits exploded, making Charles the equivalent of a billionaire in today's wealth at the time of his death in 1897. Sales reached plateau around World War I. As America urbanized, home baking and the demand for Fleischmann's Yeast fell sharply. Prohibition threw another wrench in sales, and Fleischmann's great distilleries were fired down.

The J. Walter Thompson advertising agency came to a spectacular rescue with the "Yeast for Health" campaign. Rather than rely on modest sales from a baking ingredient that was needed only in small quantities anyway, Thompson suggested that the consumer could eat the product directly, consuming maybe 2-3 cakes of yeast each day. It was learned that yeast contained vitamin B, essential for health—yeast was touted as a tonic for everything from pimples to constipation. The Federal Trade Commission, however, had some difficulty with these claims. Fortunately for Fleischmann's the "Yeast for Health" campaign overlapped the end of Prohibition, and the profitable liquor revenue stream kicked back in.

Despite the size and complexity of the business, the Fleischmann family held the reigns of the company for nearly 90 years, and was perhaps even more individualistic and colorful than conformist corporate America would wish to remember. Each generation provided solid achievements for society.

Jewish immigrants from Eastern Europe, Charles and his brothers and sisters were from a well-to-do, successful family of merchants. They landed in America with high hopes, skills, and some financial means. A man of immense energies and creative genius, Charles not only had time to patent dozens of inventions, found several businesses and a bank, he served as state senator for Ohio and cultivated a passion for horse breeding and classical piano. Feeling socially constrained by the prejudices of New York City society, he encouraged his family to build summer homes around Griffin Corners in the Catskills, which quickly attracted other Jewish vacationers and hoteliers. For the next 80 years or so, the Catskills "Borscht Belt" became a major resort destination.

Charles' son Julius became mayor of Cincinnati at age 28, owned a substantial portion of the Cincinnati Red Socks, and was the President of Cincinnati College of Music. His son Julius Jr., a.k.a. "Junkie," loved foxhunts, horses, and yachts, and helped develop Naples, Florida. Juilus Sr.'s brother Max served in the Spanish-American War, developed into a passionate yachtsman, big game hunter, balloon corps instructor, and a great philanthropist, establishing the Santa Barbara Museum of Natural History and the Nevada State Museum.

Their sister Bettie married Dr. Christian Holmes, the founder of the University of Cincinnati Medical School. She was chair of the Cincinnati Orchestra Association and wrestled with the healthy ego of conductor Leopold Stokowski. Bettie Fleischmann Holmes was an ardent collector of Asian art, and took a fancy to the psychic readings of Edgar Cayce. Her son, Christian R. Holmes II, bought himself a private island in Hawai`i—Coconut Island. With his menagerie of elephants, chimpanzees, exotic birds, tropical aquaria, and a flotilla of watercraft, Holmes entertained the Hollywood set, from Errol Flynn to Shirley Temple. To try to keep him gainfully occupied, Bettie bought him Hawaiian Tuna Packers Co., which produced well-known trade names to the American consumer, including Coral Brand Tuna and Figaro Cat Food.

Meanwhile the company marched on, becoming Standard Brands in 1929 with the addition of Royal Baking Powder, Chase & Sanborn Coffee, and the Gillette Company. Among other innovations, Standard Brands set into motion the commodification of the brand name and the separation of the brand from family operations. This paved the way for massive single companies owning a crazy quilt of brand labels, each with its own history of development. Surviving the stock market crash, the Great Depression, and World War II, Standard Brands, in the 1980s, merged with Nabisco. Soon, tobacco giant RJ Reynolds grafted its name with Nabisco. Then, in the late 1980s, the huge food conglomerates began to spin off Fleischmann products to other companies. Long after the family retired from the business, these products still carry a cache of solid product reliability and quality, as originally established and nurtured by the amazing Fleischmann family.

P. Christiaan Klieger
San Francisco

One

EMPIRE OF MICROBES

The history of Fleischmann Yeast can be summarized into several periods based on substantially different marketing approaches reflecting prevailing attitudes at the time. The first was designed, no doubt, on Charles Fleischmann's convictions that the bakeries of the Austrian Empire produced a product far superior to that in America. He felt it was primarily due to the quality of the yeast. This approach prevailed at the Philadelphia Exposition of 1876, when thousands of Americans were introduced to the pleasures of Viennese pastries, many of which could be made right at home with the proper ingredients. And that naturally included fresh Fleischmann's yeast.

Second, with the establishment of the firm and the development of extensive distribution networks, Fleischmann's approached the work of baking also as a sacrament—bread was the staff of life, nature's perfect food. The message fit hand-in-glove with the expansion of American society to the West. Home baking was often a necessity for the pioneers of the late 19th century. What better message to stress than family strength, self-reliance, and good nutrition, with home made bread serving as a link to all these values?

Third, as the country's interior began to be settled, and towns and cities grew, the convenience of neighborhood bakeries began to erode the mass market for home yeast utilization. Sales of Fleischmann Yeast to the home baking market plummeted in the first two decades of the 20th century. The advertising firm of J. Walter Thompson was hired to bring Fleischmann's Yeast back into the forefront of American consciousness. In many a household, fortunately, bread products were still considered the staff of life. Indeed, Marie Antoinette lost her head over that brioche comment, and the 1917 bread riot in Imperial Russia was a current event. As a "holy" component of well-formed American values and the keystone of well-balanced nutrition, it took very little imagination to leave out the bread and claim that the yeast itself was essential for good health. Allegedly curing everything from acne to constipation, yeast was eaten in vast quantities from 1919 to the late 1930s, when the Federal Trade Commission, backed by irate health professionals, fined Fleischmann's for apparent exaggerated claims.

During the fourth period, Fleischmann's went on to invent active dry yeast in the 1940s, just in time for World War II logistical support—for this they were lauded by the U.S. government. Convenience was early embraced in the 1950s, when Wonder Bread, Jell-O, and Birdseye frozen vegetables appeared—epiphanies to relieve overworked housewives from the drudgery of preparing endless family meals from scratch. Fleishmann's products probably seemed hopelessly old fashioned, used only by isolated farmers' wives or fragile dowagers who never got the message that eating yeast might actually be bad for you.

As the nifty '50s turned into the shaggy '60s, many a young person rediscovered nature. Wholegrain flour, golden honey and dark brown molasses matched earth-toned kitchen appliances of the 1970s, and with the revived interest in household gardens and home cooking, Fleischmann was again poised to promote baker's yeast as a fun and easy return to simple values. "Bake it Easy" resounded with the ideals of work, family, and simple, wholesome nutrition.

Until quite recently, the family and the company were closely linked, and one has to wonder which component was the more spectacular. For at least three generations the Fleischmann family excelled at everything presented them: business, music, fine art, natural science, duty to community...rarely can fault be found in the chronicle of this extraordinary family and its red and yellow brand that will always be apart of the American brand consciousness.

But it all began with the slow development of a purified yeast culture. Yeast ferments sugars contained in flour or sugary liquid, producing carbon dioxide gas and alcohol. In dough, the tiny bubbles are trapped, causing the dough to rise and become light and airy. In a liquid mixture of grains or fruit juice, some of the carbon dioxide may become dissolved with the alcohol and water, becoming a frothy beer or sparking wine.

Brewing beer and making leavened bread was developed almost as soon a grain agriculture began, perhaps 10,000 years ago in the "Fertile Crescent" of Iran-Iraq, and a few thousands of years later in China and Mexico and perhaps New Guinea. On ancient Sumerian cuneiform tablets, the epic of Gilgamesch of 3,000 B.C. described bread and brew being transformed by fermentation into food and drink fit for the gods and their earthly kings. Seamlessly, the Babylonians continued utilizing grain for baking and brewing in the region, exporting as many as 20 types of beers as far away as Egypt. Under the code of King Hammurabi (1728-1686 B.C.), the people were give daily rations of beer according to their social standing. High priests and managers got five liters per day, while workers had to contend with only two! Beer and bread making were also refined arts in ancient Egypt. Pliny the Elder of the 1st century B.C. noted that Gallic and Iberian bread was leavened with beer foam, an ingredient that no doubt supplied live yeast to the refreshingly light bread.

Fermented grain culture is also very old in Western Europe, especially in Germany where the broad plains of the northern portions of the land were ideal for growing wheat. In fact, the beer-and-bread culture is nearly synonymous with Germany itself. The earliest evidence found is a beer amphorae from Kulmbach, of the Hallsstattzweit Culture around 800 B.C. Until around 1,000 A.D., beer brewing and bread making were considered women's work. Then, monastic institutions took up brewing and selling beer. But as the cloisters could not be taxed, most were eventually secularized to insure revenue flow into the imperial and royal coffers.

In the Middle Ages, the knowledge of brewing was closely guarded by the guilds and the apprentice system. As shipping became more efficient, surplus beer production was exported as far away as India. The art developed with an appreciation for quality in ingredients and methods that was eventually codified in the Reinheitsgebot, the law for producing genuine German beer, of a quality considered fit for health and nutrition. Promulgated in 1516 by Duke Wilhelm IV of Bavaria, it stated, "the only ingredients used for the brewing of beer must be Barley, Hops, and Water. Whosoever knowingly disregards or transgresses upon this ordinance shall be punished by the Court authorities' confiscating such barrels of beer, without fail." Prior to this standardization, beer was being brewed from a hotchpotch of ingredients such as raspberries, elderberry, caraway, lavender, dandelion, bay leaves, balm, nutmeg, cherry leaves, plums, rose leaves, rosemary, juniper berries, anise, myrtle, oak leaves, lemons, and even poison ivy. When yeast was discovered to be the agent of fermentation, it was added to the Reinheitsgebot law. In following strict procedures to prevent adulteration, the Germans probably stumbled upon a method for producing pure strains of yeast. The Medieval Germans were among the first microbiologists, perhaps without realizing it. But they did understand that the key to the highest quality beer and baked goods lay in rigidly adhering customs that became the Reinheitgebot. Without these strict methods, there was no way of maintaining the uniformity of the yeast mixture. The introduction of wild yeast cells can cause uneven leavening, while septic conditions generated through sloppy handling and hygiene can introduce other fungi and bacteria into the growing media, competing with or killing the yeast.

By the end of the 18th century, two yeast strains were identified in the brewing process, the so-called "high" or top yeast (Saccharomyces cerevisiae), and "low" or bottom yeast (Saccharomyces carlsbergensis). Dutch distillers put the high yeast on the market specifically for bread making in 1780. The process of producing large quantities of pure Saccharomyces cerevisiae was established in Hanover around 1800, at the Lücke factory. This bakers' yeast was sold in the form of cream. In 1825, Tebbenhof invented the means to compress the yeast, extracting water and forming small blocks of pure yeast.

The first half of the 19th century saw the invention of two devices that would revolutionize the brewing and distilling business. James Watt invented the steam engine that could be used for efficiently firing brew houses and stills, providing a steady stream of even heat. The opposite was achieved in Carl von Linde's refrigeration system, which effectively removed heat from the fermentation process. Among other things, this allowed brewing, distilling, and yeast production to continue year round.

Also trained at the Lücke works, Herr Reiminghaus at Vienna's Mautner factory developed a process for producing mass quantities of good yeast a low cost in 1867. Using high yeast, wort was prepared such that the carbon dioxide gas carried the yeast particles to the surface, forming a foam that could be skimmed off, filtered, washed, and compressed. This became known as the Viennese process of yeast production, which is still used today as the industry standard.

In the old German Empire, beer and bread eventually comprised the bulk of the diet for most of the population. "Liquid bread" is still central to German culture, with consumers downing more than 300 liters per capita, the highest in the world. Over hundreds of years, through trial-and-error, the Germans perfected the arts of brewing and baking fine breads from the finest flour. (A)

Between 1857 and 1863, French scientist Louis Pasteur finally discovered the role of the tiny one-celled yeast fungus in the fermentation process. Saccharomyces cerevisiae is one of the tiny beasts responsible for producing some of humanity's greatest pleasures. The process is quite simple: yeast cells consume sugar, producing ethyl alcohol and carbon dioxide as waste products. Limit the presence of oxygen, such as in bread dough, and the yeast does not reproduce much but does produce large quantities of alcohol and carbon dioxide. Add a rich stream of oxygen, and the yeast uses the sugar to bud and reproduce, with limited production of waste materials. The former, anaerobic process, is used for leavening bread and fermenting beer, wine, and spirit mashes; the latter, aerobic process, is used for the commercial preparation of yeast.

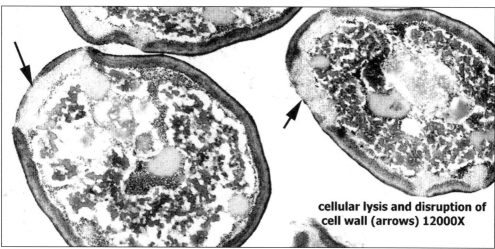

cellular lysis and disruption of cell wall (arrows) 12000X

Saccharomyces carlsbergensis was not isolated until 1883, by Hansen of Carlsberg Brewery, Copenhagen. A bottom fermentor, it is primarily used for the fermentation of lager beer. The other major yeast, Saccharomyces cerevisiae, prefers glucose as its food. The complex carbohydrates of grain cannot be reduced directly by yeast. The grain's starch first needs to be malted—then the yeast can hydrolyze the maltose sugars. Grain worts will eventually be reduced to glucose, but at a considerable sacrifice of energy and yeast reproductive productivity. Molasses, on the other hand, is a good source of simpler sucrose sugars, easily split into glucose and fructose by yeast enzymes. The addition of nitrogen, phosphate, and other nutrients also encourages the reproduction of the yeast cells. In the most efficient modern yeast production facility, a small vial of pure yeast culture can produce over 40 tons of yeast in about ten days. Needless to say, the profit potential of such a yield is tremendous.

Two

THE FOUNDERS

Knowledge of these discoveries awaited Charles Fleischmann and his brothers, who would take their knowledge of fermentation, yeast production, and distillation to America, apply just-invented technology and scientific discoveries, and proceed to make one of the largest business fortunes ever. In the United States, Charles Fleischmann is usually credited for the invention of commercially produced compressed yeast. This is not true—credit must be given to Tebbenhof and Reiminghaus. Charles and his partners' particular genius was to take the newly refined Viennese process of compressed yeast production to America, create a powerful demand for the product, and satisfy that demand with a very efficient marketing and distribution system.

Emigration to the United States was clearly on the mind of Abraham and Babette Fleischmann's children in the 1860s, especially as the Austro-Prussian War was raging and the American Civil War had just ended. When sister Josephine married in early 1866 in New York City, Max and Charles attended the wedding. Max took out naturalization papers in May of that year. In November 1866 Charles married Henriette Robertson of New York, and most likely returned to Central Europe with his bride. He applied for U.S. naturalization in August 1867. Eventually, all Abraham and Babette Fleischmann's children immigrated to America.

That Charles Fleischmann was aghast at the poor quality of baked goods in America when he first attended his sister's wedding is most likely true, but the myth that he immediately decided to do something about it is probably apocryphal. Legend relates that he instantly returned to Austria, isolated a pure strain of yeast, and returned. The great founder boldly strutted down the gangplank in New York City, humming the new, popular march from "Tannhaüser," with a tiny vial of yeast secreted in his waistcoat pocket, thus beginning the fabulous food and beverage industry. It is true, however, that Fleischmann recognized that America was far behind Europe in fermentation technology, and herein he saw a great opportunity.

Fixed or in transit, most American home bakers had struggled on with various sourdough starters, liquid concoctions of sugar, malt, flour, and potatoes, the foamy brewer's yeast skimmed from fermenting ale, or other such potions. Such elixirs were often filled with wild strains of natural yeast (often Candida milleri), in addition to other fungi and molds, and bacteria. Lactobacillus sanfrancisco is the bacteria in San Francisco sourdoughs, which hydrolyzes the maltose into carbon dioxide and acetic acid instead of alcohol. What Fleischmann perceived in the doughy Armageddon of mid-19th century America was that each microbe naturally competed to survive. Even if some leavening action was achieved by these various wild strains of yeast and bacteria, the microbeasts succeeded in adding their own waste products to the brew, resulting in unpredictable bitterness, sourness, and other off-tastes in the finished baked goods. What was certain in the founding story was that Charles and Max arrived in an America that had no commercial yeast production.

Charles and Max found work at a New York distillery that utilized the "Hungarian" process, one that was thought to be superior to other methods and the one that Charles had trained in. There they met Julius Freiberg, a successful Cincinnati distiller. Freiberg was so impressed with Charles' recent patenting of the Hungarian Process of distillation that he bought an interest in it. No doubt with the encouragement of Freiberg, the Fleischmann brothers moved to Cincinnati in 1868. This city was then the third largest manufacturing metropolis in the United States, wonderfully located on the great Ohio River, and a hub to railroads spanning the newly reunified country. It also had sizable German and Eastern European communities used to the tradition of fine European breads.

The Fleischmanns, like Freiberg, were participating in the second great wave of Jewish immigration to the United States. While early Jews settled along the Atlantic Coast, many parties who arrived after 1830 crossed the mountains into the Ohio and Mississippi valleys. Some, like Levi Strauss, headed all the way across the continent to San Francisco during the Gold Rush of 1849, peddling textiles, kitchenwares, and other non-perishables as he went along. Rarely allowed to own land, the Jews of Europe had developed great skills in itinerant trade, peddling their wares from door to door. In America, ubiquitous Jewish peddlers provided a level of consumer service in the 19th century that is rarely achieved today. This personal resourcefulness was another key to Charles Fleischmann's great success. All that the Fleischmann brothers lacked was a strong financial backer.

James Gaff was born in 1816 in Springfield, New Jersey and raised in a family of ten children. His father was a papermaker who relocated to Philadelphia. Older brother Thomas learned the distillers' trade from their uncle in New York City. Thomas returned to Philadelphia and with his brothers established a distillery there. In 1843, Thomas and James began a new distillery at Aurora, Indiana, 23 miles west of Cincinnati. This operation was quite successful, allowing for investment in brewing, farming, banking, mining, and railroads throughout the region. Popular James Gaff was even elected to the Indiana State Senate in 1859. In 1865, Gaff moved to Cincinnati and soon befriended the Fleischmann brothers.

Gaff acquired an established distillery in 1869 and renamed it James W. Gaff & Company. He also was a principal in the Memphis & Cincinnati Packet Company operating on the Ohio River, as well as the Mosler Safe Company, the Niles Tool Works, and the hardware company of Perin & Gaff. During this time the Fleischmann brothers probably became employees of Gaff. Gaff was well known as a benevolent benefactor to young men with ambitious business ideas.

During the first year of operations, yeast was grown in copper vats from a malty brew of corn, rye, barley, and sugar. When the yeast had consumed the medium and had reproduced many times, the mass would be rinsed in water and pressed through cloth into cakes. These would be wrapped in tin foil and set out immediately for sale, quite often by Charles making door-to-door sales calls. Although the foil wrapping helped protect the yeast, it could only survive a few days.

The Fleischmann brothers helped develop modern American home baking, beginning with Cincinnati's large Reform Jewish population. Another product of that city that helped develop this burgeoning American cuisine was Procter & Gamble's lard-free shortening, Crisco. Now, all-American apple pies could be baked by Jewish immigrants, in addition to fresh bread prepared with pure Fleischmann's yeast.

The Riverside plant was in operation only about one year when a night watchman's lantern exploded and the resultant fire engulfed the factory. Luckily, the partners were insured against most of the damages, and the factory was quickly rebuilt.

Gaff, Fleischmann & Co. still struggled to realize adequate yeast sales, however. While immigrants from Europe, including German settlers and Jews from Eastern Europe, readily purchased the product to produce the fine breads that they were accustomed to in the Old Country, older American families did not buy it. The few bakeries in American also were skeptical. James Gaff and the Fleischmann brothers thought that New York, with a larger and broader European immigrant market, might be a more appropriate location. Shopping around, they found an appropriate distillery at Blissville, Long Island, New York to be near that major market. However, the lease required a $100,000 indemnity bond. After inquiring for prospective partners in Cincinnati, the Fleischmann's great friend Julius Freiberg stepped forward and signed the bond. (Charles named his first-born son Julius).

A highly profitable waste product of yeast production is grain alcohol. Within two years the Fleischmanns had expanded their work in controlled fermentation to produce America's first distilled gin under the Fleischmann Distilling Company name. Even with the profitable liquor line, business grew slowly at first. The New York operation soon ran into financial difficulty, perhaps due to over-extension. Gaff and the Fleischmanns desperately needed to more successfully market their product to a larger, national audience.

They were definitely on the right course, however, when they participated in several Cincinnati industrial expositions held in the early 1870s. Here they learned how to promote their products by educating their audiences on the benefits of packaged yeast, winning bronze medals for their efforts.

The American consumer remembered the association of such wonderful bread products with Fleischmann's yeast. Charles and Max opened permanent restaurants with the "Vienna Bakery" theme in New York and Philadelphia. Brother Louis, just discharged from the Austro-Hungarian army and new to the United States, was put in charge of these operations.

Fleischmann's yeast products arrived just when pioneers from the eastern states were rapidly settling the western United States. Frontiersmen and women living out in the vast prairies and plains had to be self-reliant, and reliable products such as Fleischmann's yeast soon became essential. The Fleischmann genius could be seen in the development of a remarkable system of distribution that quickly brought the perishable product to consumers around the country. A third plant was opened at East Millstone, New Jersey with a capitalization of $600,000. When refrigerated rail cars were invented in the 1880s, Fleischmann Yeast could ship their product nearly anywhere in the country.

The keys to Gaff and Fleischmann's success was one, the reliability of the product, which had greater and more uniform leavening power than any homemade alternative and two, the capacity of the delivery service, which provided live, active yeast to their most critical customers, the commercial bakers, along with brand name recognition.

In 1879 James Gaff died, having become a major figure in American business life. As his heirs did not wish to continue the business, they sold their interest for $500,000 to the Fleischmann brothers in 1881. Max and Charles reorganized the business as a proprietorship named Fleischmann & Company. By now it had over 1,000 bakeries as clients, and untold individual customers. The brothers finally purchased the facility previously leased in New York, and Max moved to New York to manage it (he passed away there in 1891).

To avoid ending up as a dense brick during baking, most bread needs some sort of leaven. While in New England, a tradition of "salt rising bread" was part of the custom, while the South had its sour milk and saleratus for its corn pone and biscuits. Pioneers heading to the gold country of Montana and Idaho, like the '49ers of California before, still brought the old lump of sourdough starter. This was easier to carry than the bottle of liquid yeast that was then available. They baked their bread from the chuck wagons where they camped, and often left behind a blob of starter in the crotch of a tree, considerate of fellow travelers.

Charles Louis Fleischmann was born on November 3, 1834 in the little Prussian border town of Jagerndorf, (now Krnov, Czech Republic) in the Silesian mountains north of Moravia, which was then part of the Austrian Empire. Charles was the son of Abraham (Alois) and Babette Fleischmann, the second of seven children, including Josephine, Henry, Carolina, Louis, Maximillian, and Gustav. Although his father was a merchant, Charles learned about yeast early on. He left school at 13 for Prague and Vienna, where he mastered the distillery trade of under the tutelage of a Hungarian gentleman. Soon he became yeast production superintendent of the nobleman's large estate.

In 1870, James Gaff visited Europe and toured distilleries in Hungary. There he encountered a by-product of the distilleries—yeast. He sampled the breads and pastries made from this yeast and was overcome with their quality and taste. When he returned home, he immediately went to Charles Fleischmann and asked him about the yeast. "Why, I know all about that yeast," said Fleischmann, "I have made it and can make it again." Gaff responded, "Then why in the world didn't you tell me before?" (HF)

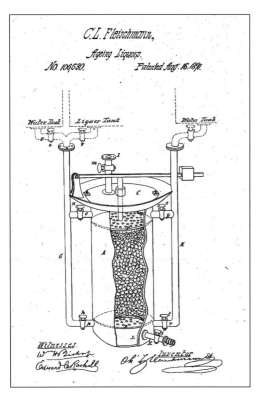

C.L. Fleischmann,
Ageing Liquors.
No. 106530.   Patented Aug. 16.1870.

Gaff and the Fleischmanns immediately discussed ideas to manufacture and distribute compressed yeast cakes. The partnership of Gaff, Fleischmann & Company was soon formed with a capitalization of $40,000. The first of Charles Fleischmann's patents, #106,530, was issued in 1870. Fleischmann attested: "The object of my invention consists in obtaining from the rectifying medium the greatest amount of rectifying power, and to abstract from the saturated coal, or other suitable material all the absorbed liquor." (U)

The second great patent—for skimming the yeast-rich froth from the top of a fermentation tank and separating the yeast from the waste materials. About this time another Fleischmann brother, Henry, arrived from Hungary and took out U.S. Patent #102,387 for the manufacture of compressed yeast. This he gave to Charles. (U)

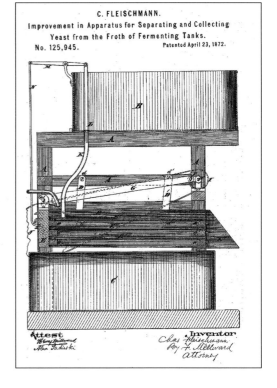

C. FLEISCHMANN.
Improvement in Apparatus for Separating and Collecting Yeast from the Froth of Fermenting Tanks.
No. 125,945.   Patented April 23, 1872.

In the spring of 1870, James and the Fleischmann brothers bought 11.89 acres of farmland along the Ohio River at Riverside, Ohio near Cincinnati for $20,000. Gaff owned 50% of the property; the brothers each held 25%. This first yeast plant in America was constructed adjacent to the Baltimore and Ohio Railroad and Ohio River at Riverside, outside of Cincinnati, for efficient transportation of raw materials and finished product. This arrangement, which was similar to Gaff's distillery in Aurora, would be utilized at many future Fleischmann plants. Charles, wishing to live conveniently near his operations, built a residence on a hill opposite the plant. (C)

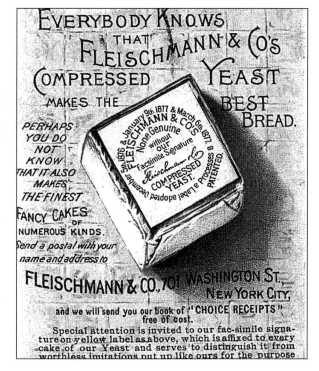

Marketing success following the Centennial Exposition was assured by a rigorous control over brand packaging—the Yellow Label with Fleischmann's signature an ominous message to beware of counterfeits. (A)

Liberal advertising through trade cards, premiums, and recipe book give-aways were also tried with great success. This is one of the first trade cards, a colorful souvenir of the purchase of a yeast cake that people kept or traded. The use of healthy-looking children in ads was a hallmark of Fleischmann's. (A)

BEWARE OF IMITATIONS
AND COUNTERFEITS OF

FLEISCHMANN & CO.'S
COMPRESSED YEAST.

THE STANDARD FOR A QUARTER OF A CENTURY.

Ours (FLEISCHMANN & CO.'S) is the only genuine Compressed Yeast in the market. Unscrupulous competitors are making a Yeast in imitation of ours, put up in the same kind of tin foil wrapper, and labelled with a label of the same color and general design as ours, with the evident intent to mislead the purchaser and to palm off their inferior goods under cover of the established reputation of our Yeast.

This timely warning is hereby given that you may protect yourself against a fraud.

DO NOT SUBMIT TO IMPOSITION. If you wish to ensure having good, light, sweet and wholesome *Bread* and the most delicious *Buckwheat Cakes, &c.*, you must insist upon getting **FLEISCHMANN & CO.'S COMPRESSED YEAST**, every cake of which bears our *Yellow Label* with fac-simile signature appearing thereon, thus:

(NONE OTHER IS GENUINE.) *Fleischmann & Co*

NOTICE. —If you will mail to us at 701 Washington Street, N. Y. City, 25 of our labels, bearing our signature, taken from our Yeast, we will mail you in exchange a handsome banner (picture) card. Write your address plainly.

Beware of Imitations! Charles Fleischmann was a pioneer in the creation of the American brand name through constant reinforcement and image protection. (A)

The Fleischmann trade card chronicled ideal life in America of the late 19th century. Charles had a particular passion for the sea. (A)

(*inset*) Gaining confidence in their marketing expertise and growing company, Gaff and the Fleischmanns gathered up a $3,000 concession fee and applied to the great Centennial Exposition to be held in Philadelphia from May to November of 1876. This world's fair was a celebration of the arts of the Industrial Revolution, and it attracted 10 million visitors. Gaff, Fleischmann established the Vienna Model Bakery concession, where they demonstrated the yeast leaving process, baked the bread, and offered guests fresh Viennese pastries, as well as coffee, ices, and chocolate. It was a smash.

Romance was also a sentimental theme during the 1870s in American advertising. (A)

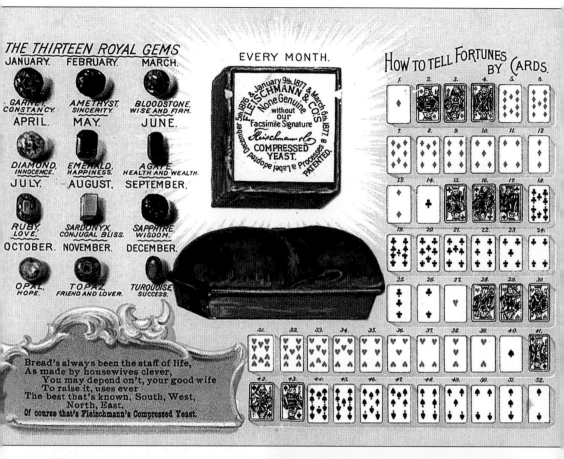

Fleischmann imagery took a light-hearted, exotic bent in its early advertising, exploring the voodoo magic of an African-American fortune teller or teaching housewives how to divine the future through reading the cards, casting dominoes, dreams, or even examining fingernails. At right is "Good luck, Honey," a lithograph by Harry Roseland, 1906, used by Fleischmann. (A) (A)

GERMAN COFFEE CAKE

For years at four the old folks treat
Is duly made a feast;
It's Coffee Cake they daily eat,
    Raised with Fleischmann's Compressed Yeast.
No wonder they partake with zest;
It is so easy to digest.

Fleischmann advertising chronicled perceptions of ethnicity as well. German-Americans, Fleischmann's initial market, were acknowledged (left), as was the cliché of the African-American "Mammy" lording over the kitchen (below). (A) (A)

AUNTY'S BREAKFAST CAKES

Oh, breakfast cakes of russet gold
    Just by the fire kissed,
Who can your charms unmoved behold?
    Who can those charms resist?
Especially are ye a feast
When raised by Fleischmann's Compressed Yeast.

Charles originally went door-to-door selling his yeast. As the business expanded, Gaff and Fleischmann hired scores of deliverymen. Eventually, with an extensive distribution network of sale agencies, the "Fleischmann Man" became a common sight plying the roads on regular routes with horse and carriage. The invention of the refrigerated railcar in the 1880s also helped distribute the product nationally. This reliability slowly won the confidence of commercial bakers. "In storm, in sunshine, rain or sleet," the Company proclaimed, "You see our wagons on the street." (A)

Bread baked with Fleischmann's yeast was touted as being so superior that even hobos would reject a competitors' product. (A)

27

By all accounts the Fleischmanns were a happy family. Charles and Henriette Fleischmann, shown here, had a daughter Bettie (b. 1871) and two sons, Julius (b. 1872) and Max (b. 1877). The children were raised as Unitarian Christians. Papa Fleischmann was a great natural musician, and could play any tune on the piano by ear. He encouraged his children to play music and sing. His children and many grandchildren went on to become passionate patrons of the opera, ballet, stage, and symphony, while a nephew became a famous publisher. (N)

Charles constructed a mansion on Washington Street in the leafy Cincinnati district of Avondale. By the 1890s Charles Fleischmann had four production plants, vacation homes, a yacht, a stable of racehorses, and was a state senator to boot. Famed jockey Tod Sloane managed his stables, which produced many champions. Charles became a "Kentucky" Colonel in 1890 through appointment to the staff of William McKinley, who was then governor of Ohio and a close friend. Fleischmann gave a horse to him when he became president. (C)

Suffering from respiratory problems, Charles Fleischmann was encouraged by his doctors to remain outdoors as much as possible. The family soon discovered the beautiful Catskill Mountains in New York. Charles bought 60 acres west of Griffin Corners in 1883 from local businessman John Blish. Turning Griffin Corners into a monument of gracious living—not far from New York City—attracted other individuals of Jewish ancestry who were snubbed by society watering holes elsewhere, and other mansions and hotels followed. In 1906 Lake Switzerland was built for boating and swimming, and to harvest ice in the winter. Later, summer stock entertainers, Vaudeville comedians, and other primarily Jewish stars like hometown girl Molly Goldberg entertained at the lavish hotels that had been built—it was now known as the famous "Borscht Belt" for all the summer residents of Eastern European ancestry. Herbert Lehman, Governor of New York, the Leibman family, and the conductor Anton Seidel had summer homes here. In honor of Papa and Julius Fleischmann, the town's name was changed to "Fleischmanns." (A)

The elder Fleischmann built a large mansion up in the surrounding hills, near the Ulster & Delaware Railroad station. It had broad porches, turrets, and terraces, and was surrounded by a deer park, riding stable, baseball field, a heated pool filled with spring water, and a stocked trout pond. His relatives built homes of their own forming a family complex, and other families soon joined building great summer homes. The Fleischmann estate was later developed into a hotel. (S)

29

The Fleischmann family arrived in the Catskills on their holidays in private rail cars from their yachts anchored at the mouth of the Rondout River. At the station, their own marching band decked-out in the Fleischmann livery greeted them. This band also played at the summer baseball games, where professional baseball stars played incognito and Max and Julius joined in too. The Fleischmann brothers were known to entertain the public by riding standing up and performing other equestrian feats. (A)

But despite all the outdoor life, Papa Fleischmann's health began to fade. When he caught pneumonia in 1891, a young doctor named Christian R. Holmes attended to Charles Fleischmann. This young Dane would become his son-in-law. But in 1897, at the age of 63, Charles passed away—only then did his wonderful philanthropy become known. In 1893 Charles had saved his Market National Bank when it was discovered that a cashier had embezzled $160,000. Rather than having a run on the bank, Fleischmann paid the shortage out of his own pocket, and took a deed on the man's house. After the cashier's death, he gave the house back to the man's widow. Charles Fleischmann was buried in a magnificent Greek temple in Central Cincinnati near the University.

30

Three

JULIUS FLEISCHMANN

The second generation of Fleischmanns learned the art of living well from Charles. The two brothers Julius and Max, and elder sister Bettie were, in there own ways, as talented as their father was. Each had a commanding personality, each had a passion for collecting, a love of music and adventure, and each understood that great wealth incurred a social responsibility to the enrichment of the culture of their community and the welfare of its inhabitants.

Julius was born in 1872 soon after the yeast factory and distillery was rebuilt at Riverside. He was educated in Cincinnati public schools, but left Hughes High School at 15 to join Franklin Preparatory School. However, rather than enter college, he joined his father's firm at 16 as a clerk. He did very well under his father's exacting supervision. In a short time he would assume the entire management of the company. In 1893 he married Lily Ackerland. The couple had three children: Louise, Charles, and Julius Jr. Larger than life, this bon vivant persona seems to have been a prototype for Fitzgerald's Great Gatsby. Whereas F.W. Woolworth and J.C. Penney may have had more money, no one quite had the style of the second-generation Fleischmanns.

Julius Fleischmann vigorously promoted Cincinnati's extensive rail network, no doubt remembering the importance of superior transportation and distribution facilities to the success of the company founded by his father. During his administration as mayor, the city police force was considered one of the best in the nation. Very much the Republican plutocrat, Julius proclaimed:

Cincinnati's economical and progressive administration is one of the vastest importance in bringing new enterprises to the city, and in advancing the interests which for so many years have made Cincinnati so justly famed for her commercial soundness and integrity. It is to the city which is well governed, and whose financial interests are managed as a prudent businessman would care for his private investments, that capital is attracted.

Fleischmann annexed suburban districts, created parks, opened free public baths, and initiated an educational renaissance. This was all done despite the ravages of Boss Cox's political machine that dominated Cincinnati politics. Julius Fleischmann also served as an aide to Governors Bushnell and Nash, and was a G.O.P. convention delegate in 1904, 1908, and 1912.

A matchless over-achiever, Julius was not only mayor of Cincinnati and president of Fleischmann & Co., he was president of the Market National Bank, Cincinnati College of Music, Union Grain and Hay Company, Riverside Malting and Elevator Company, Illinois Vinegar Manufacturing Company of Chicago, Cincinnati Athletic Club, Security Savings Bank and Safe Deposit Company, and a governor of the Queen City Club. He was a member of the Cincinnati Chamber of Commerce, the Manufacturing Club, Business Men's Club, Commercial Club, Optimist Club, Walnut Hills Business Men's Club, Phoenix Club,

Cincinnati Country Club, Riding Club, Young Men's Blain Club, Stamina Republican League, Avon Lodge, No. 542, F. &A.M., and the North Cincinnati Turnverein. He was a 32nd-degree Mason and a Shriner, in addition to being a member of the Royal Arcanum, Knights of Pythias, and the Elks. He was vice-president of the C.N. & C. Railroad, and had interests in the South Covington & Cincinnati Street Railway Company before he was mayor. With brother Max, he owned the Cincinnati Red Socks Baseball Club.

Julius was a pioneer in the adoption of the automobile. In 1901 he drove, with his chauffeur Joe Brydges, an amazing 1,200 miles from Avondale to Fleischmanns, New York. The epic trip took ten days, and set a record by driving over stage roads that heretofore had only known horse and carriage. Here Julius (right, front) is shown with Brydges. In the back seat (from left) are Julius' wife Lily, his brother Max, and Max's wife Sarah, albeit on a less ambitious jaunt. (C)

From his early years, Julius was passionate about serving the Republican Party. In 1894 he was appointed aide-de-camp of Governor William McKinley, taking over that role from his aging father. In a few years McKinley went on to the White House and Julius was elected mayor of Cincinnati, the youngest ever at age 28. A consummate executive and plutocrat, but well-beloved by the electorate, he was re-elected in 1903. (Bushnell cartoon—C)

As if he had time for anything other than work, Julius was an avid sportsman. He inherited his father's superb stable and interest in horseracing. Like most Fleischmanns, he loved maritime pursuits and in 1897 took delivery of a palatial steam powered yacht, the Hiawatha, which probably had been ordered by his late father. One of the largest private vessels of its time, the ship would be the first of many owned by the Fleischmann sons and grandsons. This 138-foot long vessel was designed by Charles Seabury and built by G.E. & P. and Seabury Co. of Morris Heights, NY. Julius became a member of the New York and other yacht clubs. (M)

Julius Fleischmann built a large park in Fleischmanns, NY as a training camp for the Cincinnati Red Socks and the local Fleischmann team. One of the men on the latter was Honus Wagner, a famous major leaguer in his time. Julius gave the park to the town in 1914 with the stipulation that it always be a baseball park and that it always be free. Julius is shown here with one of his teams; Brother Max is front row, second from left. (N)

Luxury hotels in Fleischmanns included the likes of the Takanassee with its golf course and huge pool, the Terrace Hall with its own orchestra, and the majestic Grand Hotel seen here at nearby Pine Hill. Most of the hotels' staffs, sensitive to the dietary needs of their Orthodox Jewish customers, were well-trained in Kosher practices and the preparation of Eastern European favorites. The breakfasts of kippers and latkes, the cozy bungalows, the lazy afternoon row across the lake—these were all part of the summer idyll in the Catskills first created by the Fleischmann family, an age now passed.

Julius Fleischmann's Winding Hill estate in Cincinnati was located in Indian Hill, an exclusive area outside of town. Julius originally started with 21 square miles of farm land (1,600 acres), later reduced to 343 acres. Construction began in 1924 and finished three years later. It was built of Ordovician limestone quarried on the property. The estate took upwards of 37 servants to maintain. It has one-inch slate tiles on the roof and a climate-controlled room for the pipe organ. The gutters were solid lead. Wine cellars, indoor pool, ballroom—the floors were walnut. Everything about the house was an example of understated elegance. Next door was Peterloon, the 1,000-acre estate owned by John Emery. These two estates ushered in strict zoning laws, which helped create a paradise of bridle paths and stables. Here, Julius established the famous Camargo Fox Hunt. In later years, another Cincinnati Reds owner, Marge Schott, would live nearby. (G)

To Julius and his ceaseless energy is credited the transformation of Fleischmann's from a mom-and-pop operation to one of the world's industrial giants. Julius married for a second time in 1920 to Laura G. Hemingway, and a third time to a 'Ms. O'Brien.' In 1925, Julius dropped dead in Florida while playing polo. His brother Max immediately assumed the leadership of The Fleischmann Company. Major Max had received the news by runners while on safari in Africa. (C)

Four

MAX FLEISCHMANN

As Julius was the elegant dandy, his younger brother Max was the tough outdoorsman. Although they shared many interests, Max's all-consuming passion was for adventure—travel to exotic lands, big game hunting, sailing the high seas. If fact, Max had little of the taste for business that his brother and father shared. Max Fleischmann became superintendent of the manufactory department, and in agreement with his brother, the less demanding job of vice president so he could have more free time for his expeditions. Yet in the midst of an African safari, runners brought word to him of his brother's sudden death. Max took the Aquitania home, and drove directly from the docks in New York to the boardroom on Washington Street, where he was elected Chairman of The Fleischmann Company.

Some of the personality of the Major can be realized in his journals. From his polar adventure:

Two in the morning…the midnight sun—a ball of fire just over the skyline, all its radial lines cut by the fog—created a scene which baffled the pen for its beauty. Distant icebergs near the sky line glinted and glimmered, while the drift ice, on which two seals appeared, was heavier than is usually found here…there was not one dull moment of the trip.

The party sailed within 600 miles of the North Pole. The eventually caught a polar bear cub, which ended up, of course, at Cincinnati Zoo.

Two months after their arrival home Max was planning a safari to British East Africa. That party included 64 porters, cooks, gun-bearers, and horse tenders. Max and Sarah witness the battle between a rhinoceros and crocodile, and gazed in amazement as another rhino charged a train. The Zoo received a lion cub, an antelope, and a lemur, and Max collected trophies of a buffalo, waterbuck, warthog, and impala. He returned to Africa in October. The next year Max headed for the north again—this time to Alaska. In 1910 he went to Ethiopia, where he wrote in his journal:

We reached to the village of Domi-N'yuki, a powerful Meru chieftain supposed to be able to muster twenty thousand warriors in a very short time. Domi-N'yuki made us a formal visit accompanied by his body-guard and swarms of natives. The body-guard consisted of several companies of warriors, all in all, about four hundred men, armed with spears, skins around their waist, anklets of Colobus monkey, and the leader wearing leopard skins and other types of head-dresses.

Max was a hardy outdoorsman, with a macho attitude much like his friend Teddy Roosevelt. But woe be to the employee who erred:

I was very much put out as my second gun bearer lost the sight protector of my rifle. This is inexcusable carelessness on the part of a gun bearer and something that could not be overlooked for the sake of discipline and morale. He was therefore given a proper hearing to get his side of the case and then severely punished.

This trip was followed by the Altai Mountains and Outer Mongolia, where Max and Sarah, a valet, Ernest Hughes, and Abbas, another servant, took the new Trans-Siberian Railway from imperial St. Petersburg. At a stop along the way, Max again showed his sensitive side:

We spent the morning wandering about the native market. We bought a lot of wild strawberries, which are sold by the peasants for a song, and are put up in very tasty birch bark boxes.

Northeastern Rhodesia was on the itinerary for 1914. Between trips Max handled his business affairs capably. With Julius as president of most family business concerns, Max occupied the vice presidency of the main company and the Illinois Vinegar, Fleischmann Malting Company, American Diamalt, and was a director of his father's Market National Bank. Like Julius, he was a 32nd-degree Mason and a Shriner, an Elk, and a member of the Queen City Club.

Upon assuming the chairmanship of The Fleischmann Company, Max stipulated that he wished to continue to reside primarily in Santa Barbara. To expedite matters, he took Julius Bergen, Julius Fleischmann's secretary, to California to be executive secretary to the new chairman. He also purchased a private railroad car for his necessary trips between California and New York. In 1935 he bought a Lockheed aircraft to speed him on his numerous trips.

Generous to a fault, Major Max, as he was now called, drew together 25 civic-minded businessmen in 1928 to create the Santa Barbara Foundation, endowed with large gifts of company stock. Its original purpose was to endow support for free band concerts—a Fleischmann tradition hailing back to the Catskills days—it later grew to become one of the largest community foundations in the country. Max also rebuilt the crumbling Santa Barbara church, Queen of the Missions, with his own funds, and supplied funds for the Peabody football stadium at Santa Barbara High. He developed the Fleischmann Polo Field in Carptinteria.

Max Fleischmann also sponsored a major collecting trip to Southeast Asia by the American Museum of Natural History, acquiring among other animals the wild oxen called bantaung and the gigantic ghaur. Max and Sarah returned in 1938 to collect a tiger for the New York museum. Sarah shot her own tiger in Cambodia.

Max was the epitome of the gentlemen-explorer, and became a fellow of the Royal Geographic Society and the Explorers Club. He was president of the Western Museum Conference, a director of Ducks Unlimited, and trustee of Save-the-Redwoods. He owned 8,000-acre Hope Plantation in South Carolina, 40 miles outside of Charleston, with a Spanish moss-laden antebellum mansion, acres of cornfields, and 50 hunting dogs. Original Currier and Ives art covered the walls. His love for hunting and hunting dogs was perhaps one reason Fleischmann's Gin used them in their magazine advertising for so many years. He was a good friend of Teddy Roosevelt, William Boeing, and renowned sportsman Jimmy Robinson.

In 1934 and '35 the Major began to acquire land in Nevada, disgusted with high taxes in California. He built a wonderful residence at Glenbrook on Lake Tahoe, and bought the 200,000-acre Morgan Ranch, a 30,000-acre ranch in Jacks Valley, and the Ladino dairy farm near Reno. He soon applied the largess of Fleischmann philanthropy to his new Nevada home, building a summer camp for the Boy Scouts and endowing scholarships for the University of Nevada. He also gave the college the dairy farm.

After relocating to Nevada, the Major found an interest in the Nevada State Museum in Carson City. The Old U.S. Mint building was being refurbished for a museum. The Major came up with a substantial gift, and sent those planning the museum to Santa Barbara to check on his other museum of natural history. In 1941, the Nevada State Museum was opened, with Max as honorary director. A history of Nevada mining was in the basement; a hall of birds above.

Max Fleischmann, Charles' younger son, went to Riverside public schools and the Ohio Military Institute. Like his brother, he was very interested in baseball and also was an amateur boxer and a superb tennis player. And like his brother, Max was put to work in the yeast factory, first shoveling coal into the great furnaces. (N)

When Max (far left) graduated in 1896, he signed up for the Ohio National Guard and received a commission as second lieutenant, and soon went off to the Spanish American War and became aide-de-camp to Brigadier General Louis Carpenter. He served well in the war, returning late in 1898 to the family business. (N)

Max married Cincinnati's Sarah Hamilton Sherlock in December 1905 and almost immediately began to plan an expedition-honeymoon—to the Arctic Ocean! The Laura set sail that June from Norway to explore Franz Joseph fjord in Greenland, to advance to King William's Land, and to collect bird specimens and study their habits. The party was also to trying to collect a musk-ox and polar bear alive. In addition to Sarah (right), Max was accompanied by his sister Bettie (center), her husband Dr. Christian Holmes (left—who conveniently spoke Danish), their son Carl (second from left), and English friend Joel Livingstone Learmonth (second from right). (N)

Max was one of the country's first balloonists. When World War I broke out, he received a commission as captain of the Signal Officers' Reserve Corps, Balloon Branch. He became a major and commandant of the Army Aeronautical School in France. On November 1, 1918, 199 balloon officers and 623 enlisted men graduated from the school. Max had been grounded after having been gassed by the enemy, and was sent to lead the U.S. Army Balloon School in Arcadia, California. Here he and Sarah fell in love with California, especially Santa Barbara, where in 1921 they bought a ranch, built a home, and began raising lemons and avocado. As passionate about horses and polo as his father and brother, Max amassed three polo fields around Santa Barbara. Edgewood Ranch was the beginning of the "West Coast" Fleischmanns.

Max's spirit of adventure was nowhere captured as it was it his own museum, the Santa Barbara Museum of Natural History. In 1934, after many years of service on the board, he was elected president. The library of the museum was originally Max's private library—its trophy heads collected on his numerous expeditions. He created the Department of mammalogy and constructed the Sarah H. Fleischmann Bird Hall. Artifacts from the coastal tribes from Alaska and British Columbia lined the auditorium's walls. He remained as president until 1947, then continued on the board as director and executive vice president. (SB)

Max, following family tradition, was deeply involved in yachting, in fact owning 22 in his lifetime. The most spectacular were the Haida series, named after the seafaring tribe of the Queen Charlotte Islands. The great seagoing Diesel Haida was 127 feet long and included a laboratory, aquarium, darkroom, a good amount of fishing tackle, and small launches. It was designed as a scientific research vessel, albeit a very luxurious one, and was staffed by a crew of 17. To shelter it, he built a massive breakwater at Santa Barbara, which thus far had been open water. Later he joined forces with the WPA to extend the breakwater to the beach, which apparently led to beach erosion at nearby Montecito. (N)

Despite its research assignment, the Haida was not sparing in comfort. Scientists on board the Haida discovered new species and contributed significantly to the growing research publications of the Santa Barbara Museum of Natural History. Notable was a book produced by Dr. Lionel Walford on marine game fishes of the Pacific Coast. (N)

When World War II broke out, Max gave the Haida and his Lockheed aircraft to the war effort. He tried to get a commission with the services, but was ruled out because of his age. At the end of the war, he purchased a new Lockheed, which he named Silver Falcon. In the late 1940s, he took to patrolling a dangerous section of highway between his Lake Tahoe home and Zephyr Cove. He painted a Nevada State Police insignia on his car, installed a siren and flashing red lights, and began to hand out citations and warnings. Surprisingly, the number of traffic accidents was reduced on the road. When he wasn't working highway patrol, time was usually spent hunting or fishing. Max became ill on a trip to Alaska aboard the Haida in 1951. He returned to Santa Barbara where he was diagnosed with pancreatic cancer. He did not wait for the inevitable end, but ended his life on October 16, aged 74. (N)

The Fleischmann Planetarium at the University of Nevada-Reno was built with gifts from Max's foundations. In his will, the Major gave large cash gifts to his secretary Hugo Oswald, to his cousin Paul Fleischmann of New York, to his wife's nephews and nieces. For the rest of his family, he dictated "all are possessed of abundant wealth, having more than sufficient for their needs. After Sarah, the bulk of the estate went to the Santa Barbara and Max C. Fleischmann foundations. Both foundations continued the philanthropic work of their founder, with the University of Nevada the major beneficiary. In 1960 Sarah Fleischmann passed away, and according to the terms of Max Fleischmann's will, the foundation itself was liquidated 20 years later in 1980, having given away a total of $192,037,457.82. (N)

Five

BETTIE FLEISCHMANN HOLMES

Charles and Henrietta's oldest child was Bettie, born just after the first yeast factory fire. She inherited her father's huge blue eyes and musical talents, and over time developed a forceful personality and a passion for art collecting. Like the two Fleischmann sons, Bettie was educated in the local public schools. When Dr. Christian Holmes he began to visit his patient Charles Fleischmann at the Fleischmanns' Avondale home, the physician's devotion made a big impression on Charles' spirited daughter Bettie. Bettie married the devoted doctor the next year, in 1892. Despite her father's great wealth, though, Bettie only received an allowance of $100 a month well into her marriage. (C)

Christian Rasmus Holmes was the son of the miller Holm Christensen and Karen Mikkelsen of Engom, Denmark. (The name was transposed by immigration agents, and after a stint in Canada, Christian settled in Cincinnati). (F)

During the first years of the 20th century, Christian, Sr. and Bettie first operated a small, private hospital in downtown Cincinnati. Bettie saw to the operation of the hospital furnishings, meals, and general housekeeping. (F)

In due time Carl Holmes was born. On June 13, 1896, Bettie Fleischmann Holmes gave birth to their second son, Christian (left, center). In 1900, a third son, Julius, known as Jay, was born to Bettie and Christian. When Bettie, Christian Sr., and Carl accompanied her brother Max on an arctic expedition to Spitsbergen, Norway aboard the S.S.Laura in 1906, Bettie kept a journal of the voyage that she eventually published. (N)

By now Christian Sr. was a professor of otology at the Miami Medical College in Cincinnati. The Holmes lived at 3598 Washington Avenue, the home of Bettie's mother and late father. (C)

An accomplished musician like her father, Mrs. Holmes became president of the Cincinnati Orchestra Association, following the heels of Mrs. William Howard Taft who went off to become First Lady in Washington. Bettie always had forceful opinions. In 1912, she argued with the renowned conductor of the Cincinnati Symphony Orchestra, Leopold Stokowski, over "artistic differences." When she balked at releasing him from his contract, he wrote back a scathing letter: "I therefore demand of Mrs. C.R. Holmes…a recognition and fulfillment on the compact under which I signed my existing legal contract with the Cincinnati Symphony Orchestra, and that she as President of the Orchestra Association, should grant me the full and unqualified release from my legal contract…which…is my right to demand." The hissy fit ultimately resulted in the departure of Maestro from his post with the symphony. He went on to New York and continued his brilliant career.

In 1914, Dr. Holmes became Dean of the College of the University of Cincinnati. With Fleischmann philanthropy and political clout, Christian Sr. succeeded in establishing a teaching hospital, Cincinnati General. With his brother-in-law Julius, now mayor, Holmes lobbied the state legislature for support of various projects benefiting their city. Dr. Holmes, with the passionate help of wife and brother-in-law, can be credited with founding the University of Cincinnati Medical School, then the finest in the country. Both Julius and Christian stepped forth with scholarship money for bright medical students.

Carl lingered on in Paris after the armistice, attending Pasteur Institut lectures on yeast, malting, and vinegar, learning the latest from the scientific discoveries that helped motivate his grandfather. Holmes senior worked himself to death creating Cincinnati General Hospital and the medical school—in 1919 he developed cancer and passed away in January, 1920.

In New York, Bettie became committed to beautiful Sands Point (Port Washington), Long Island around 1927. Her brother Max had a residence there. Her other brother Julius had also built an estate, the "Lindens" on the Point in 1910 (and became head of the local yacht club), and her cousin Raoul Fleischmann also had a summer home. The second original Fleischmann factory was nearby. The great plant at Peekskill itself was only about two hour's drive. A secluded district in the wooded hills around Port Washington, Sands Point was protected from the harsh beachfront environment that Mrs. Holmes disliked. Enchanted by Sands Point and its relative convenience to New York City, she brought together 24.5 acres with the purchase of 17 parcels.

Prohibition in the United States was a severe blow to the great distilleries of the Fleischmann Company, which survived largely through Herculean efforts of a superb management team, superior distribution, a "Yeast for Health" ad campaign, and Bettie's campaigning. As a social activist and a promoter of Fleischmann Company interests, Mrs. Holmes helped pioneer the repeal of the 18th Amendment (the Volstead Act) in 1933. Prominent in the Women's Organization for National Prohibition Reform, her feisty pen wrote:

The fact that the published list of sponsors contains the names of some of the most highly respected women in the country inspires confidence in those who have wanted to join us, but did not dare. They are no longer afraid to come into the open and declare themselves.

Since moving permanently to New York, Bettie continued her generous philanthropy, art collecting, and active life in social and musical circles. She became a director of the New York Philharmonic Symphony Society, founded the Christian R. Holmes Foundation, and served on the board of the Metropolitan Opera Guild. The only daughter of Charles and Henriette Fleischmann died at the Chimneys, her incredible home at Sands Point, Long Island, on September 29, 1941.

Bettie's three soldiers—Dr. Holmes and his two adult sons served in World War I. Christian Sr. received a commission as a major and established a otolaryngology clinic at Fort Sherman in Ohio, while Bettie built a recreation center for officers at Chillicothe, the first of several transformations of Holmes' properties for the benefit of men serving in wartime. (F)

In 1925, Bettie constructed the Christian R. Holmes Hospital at the University of Cincinnati, following the ideal of the private hospital concept from Dr. Holmes' early practice. She underwrote the project largely with her own funds. Now a young widow, Mrs. Holmes continued her charitable work with the hospital and her service as chairwoman of the board of the Cincinnati Orchestra Association. Henriette Robertson Fleischmann, her mother, passed away in 1924. With her mother gone, Bettie left Cincinnati for good soon after the hospital was finished. She donated her father's mansion on Washington Street in Avondale to the city. Today the mansion has been demolished, but the trees and lawns live on as Fleischmann's Gardens Park. (A)

The Gold Coast was to the second generation of Fleischmanns what the Catskills were to the first. While there are hundreds of great mansions along Long Island's magnificent northern coast, few were built like Bettie Fleischmann Holmes' "Chimneys." In typical Fleischmann manner, she built her 42-room palace to last. Constructed of poured concrete over a steel frame, her indestructible home was finished in a delicate Tudor style, contrasted with wrought iron candelabra, leaden mullions, oak beams, carved walnut paneling, with carved fireplaces and entire floors scrounged from medieval European castles. (A)

Construction of the Chimneys began in 1929, the momentous year for The Fleischmann Company. Architect Edgar Williams designed what became one of the most-lauded adaptations of 16th century English Tudor architecture in the country. The Chimneys required a staff of 40-60, and most were paid a generous wage of $5.00 a day. Outlying buildings included houses for gardeners and other staff and a large guesthouse that would qualify as a substantial residence in the neighborhood in its own right. Every major room in the main three-story mansion had a fireplace, hence the name. The residence costs over $3 million, and had unheard of new technology: central air conditioning and vacuum systems, and built-in fire hoses. The Chimneys was to a large extent the prototype for her son Christian's two homes on O`ahu in distant Hawai`i—Queen's Surf and Coconut Island. (A)

In the basement, which is itself a historic site, is one of the country's first private recreation centers. It had a bowling alley, steam baths, a huge indoor pool, a racquetball court, a bar, a shooting gallery, and Art Deco mirrored dressing rooms. Although now in disuse, many of the mural paintings of exotic tropical jungle scenes and most of the fixtures are still intact. (A)

(*above, right*) To fill her mansion, Bettie spent passionate years collecting the furnishings abroad. She amassed one of the greatest collections of ancient Chinese bronzes anywhere—much of it ending up in the Avery Brundage Collection of the Asian Art Museum in San Francisco. While most of the mansion's furnishings were French or English 16th-17th century, much of the wood carvings were done by contemporary English craftsmen utilizing American hardwoods. The centerpiece of the entrance hall was a carved mast from a clipper ship built in 1772 that supports a spiral stairway leading upstairs. The nautical theme, yachting being the paramount Fleischmann passion, is carried through on the stained glass windows around the entrance. The main hall of the Chimneys is right out of Hampton Court, with its beamed ceiling and carved mantle pieces and an aeolian pipe organ. The original furniture made of dark woods and the heirloom tapestries are gone now, but in many places, the original wallpaper can be found. (A)

Bettie's brother Max was an excellent marksman, and her son Christian loved mechanical shooting galleries. Unused for perhaps 65 years, the ducks and wheels give silent testimony to the light-hearted fun of the Fleischmann-Holmes family. (A)

Six
A Changing Market

In 1911-1912, Julius realized that the future of the company lay with the growing urban population. Cities have bakeries and herein lay Julius' attention. In 1911, he opened the Fleischmann School for bakers in the Bronx, New York City. A four-week course was taught under the guidance of Joseph Backmann, and over time 3,000 bakers would benefit from this intensive program. Fleischmann's also developed a traveling school for bakers, equipping two wagons with canvas covers, ranges, hoods, mixers. The company rented vacant lots and Fleischmann agents instructed local bakers on the scientific demands of quality baking. Home economic classes were held at high schools and colleges, and students participated in baking contests.

In essence, Julius would turn a family-run business into a complex food conglomerate of international renown, building upon the brand name ideas of his father and consistent product quality. The core of Julius' operating philosophy was that "There can be no such thing as too much real service in business." In 1921 the Company created the Retail Bakery Sale Advisors, a cadre of traveling baking instructors, to help bakers in advertising, marketing, and training. A sure cure for poisons that collect in the body, Fleischmann's yeast was also just the thing for "coated tongue, bad breath, bad skin." It was the miracle drug of the Depression, Lucy's "Vita-Veeta-Vegemin" for the 1920s—not only good for you but also as smooth and rich as chocolate.

Tasty yeast is tempting
To your appetite
Creamy wholesome candy
Try a luscious bite
Vitamins are hiding
In this candy bar
Pep, vim, and vigor
Linger where they are.

Children like this lovely
Creamy food delight
Let them eat it daily
Every morning, noon and night
You will see them growing
Stronger every day
Taking yeast this handy
Dandy candy way.

With the founder's energetic sons Julius, then Max at the helm, assisted by nephews Jay, Carl, and Chris Holmes, and the power of the "Yeast for Health" ad campaign, Fleischmann sales skyrocketed in the early post-World War I years. Per capita sales jumped from 0.933 pounds in 1919 to 2.45 in 1925, a clear indication that the campaign was a roaring success. By 1925, the company had 12 plants and 2,500 sales agents, including women, a progressive idea for the time. In 1926, the Fleischmann Company was in the top ten of American magazine advertising purchasers. From 1917 to 1924, sales of yeast tripled. The company even began selling a dry yeast as a supplement in animal feed. Supplying the needs of bakers increased when "eat more muffins and cake" was added to the "Eat More Bread" campaign. By 1928 Fleischmann's held 93.4% of the business—they could no longer grow by taking sales away from competition, but had to create a new demand altogether, and the "Yeast for Health" campaign was ideally suited. Root beer, and other kinds of beer, not to mention wine and 'moonshine' could readily be made with Fleischmann's Yeast during Prohibition.

In 1931 the Federal Trade Commission stepped in to investigate most of the more blatant health claims of Fleischmann's yeast. The FTC collected testimony, and J. Walter Thompson Agency and the Fleischmann Company did the same. The government agency considered such tainted endorsements misleading to the public, especially since most of them advanced medical claims. Many testimonials were staged, the FTC complaint alleged, "the use of pictures of endorsers by respondents in which the subjects thereof are pictured as in different social class or of different standing from what they actually are." Consumer advertising was moving from the snake-oil touts of carnival barkers to much more subtle manipulation of the message, and the FTC was obviously being very cautions about the manner in which testimonials were gathered.

The huge Fleischmann ad campaign had created a new demand for a product whose original function had become a bit obsolete—but finally Fleischmann's agreed "to cease representing that the product will cure or prevent constipation, bad breath, boils, acne, pimples or other manifestations of irregular digestion…" One of many Fleischmann ironies is that the Company found itself at odds with the medical community that in Cincinnati had been so prominently supported by the Fleischmann-Holmes family. Yet the "Yeast for Health" campaign continued well into the late 1930s, boosting sales of the small foil-wrapped yeast packets from less than $1 million in the early 1920s to about $10 million by 1937.

Julius Fleischmann had set into motion a set of market expansions that took advantage of the tremendous brand value of Fleischmann's Yeast. Having saturated the market, the next logical step was to diversify into other product lines. Julius' death in 1925 put Max in charge and Joseph Wilshire of Cincinnati became president. Given that the Major preferred to live in Santa Barbara, a great expansion of the business would have taken even more of his time away from his travels, museums, foundations, and interests elsewhere. Julius Fleischmann Jr., Carl, Jay, and Chris Holmes were not interested in running the business, and Max had no children. According to family knowledge, there was no longer a compelling need for a Fleischmann to run what for so long was a family business, especially without Charles Fleischmann II, who had been the rising star. Max therefore contracted J.P. Morgan to orchestrate a merger that would bring in new products; he did not entirely remove family control of the original company, however.

New York had become the primary focus of Fleischmann's operations in 1900 when the gigantic Peekskill factory at Charles Point on the Hudson River was built (the Point was named for Julius' father). Like the original plant in Cincinnati, it was built on a navigable river and major railroad (New York Central) for convenient shipping. Before dried yeast, the live compressed yeast packets had to be delivered quickly, and the Peekskill Plant was only about an hour from New York City by express train. Large ships bringing grain or molasses could off-load at the Peekskill factory. (P)

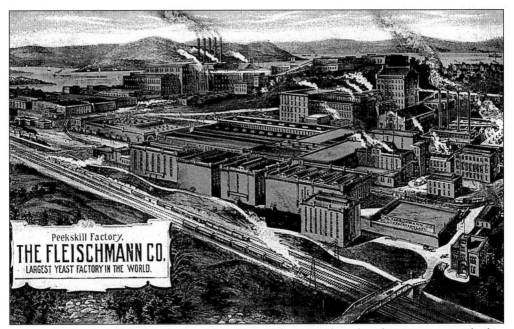

Eventually the Peekskill plant had nearly 1,000 employees and produced gin, vinegar, and other products in addition to yeast. (A)

Storage tanks at Peekskill held the millions of pounds of yeast, huge amounts of vinegar, and train loads of gin that flowed out of this small river town in New York. After 1929, Royal Gelatin and Chase and Sanborn Coffee would be added to the list. (A)

Fleischmann's, long a family proprietorship, finally incorporated in 1905, becoming The Fleischmann Company. At its peak, Fleischmann's had 12 plants and 1,000 agencies with "yeast men" servicing over 30,000 bakers and 225,000 grocers. The yeast agents would personally visit bakeries, in the middle of the night if necessary, as freshness became an obsession. (A)

Fleischmann's primary product, simple yeast, was marketed from the Gay Nineties to the Flapper era with images of grandmother's warm biscuits and happy, wholesome children with rosy, glowing cheeks. Bread made from Fleischmann's yeast was touted as the perfect food, as natural as mother's milk: "Don't be severe with hungry, growing people when they can't wait for meals. The Bread-eating habit is one to be encouraged. It's Nature's own way of saying: I'm growing. I need just lots and lots of my own food-- Bread." (A)

Root Beer, the finest summer draught
That ever slaked man's thirst,
By grateful millions daily quaffed,
As made by matrons versed,
Owes all its life—and 'tis a feast,
To Fleischmann's Peerless Compressed Yeast.

And if that didn't work, you could make them root beer. (A)

EXQUISITE DOUGHNUTS

1 cake FLEISCHMANN'S YEAST.	2 eggs.
1 cup lukewarm milk.	1½ tablespoonfuls butter.
2 tablespoonfuls lukewarm water.	½ cup light brown sugar.
2½ pints sifted flour.	¼ teaspoonful salt.
½ teaspoonful mace.	

Dissolve the Yeast in the lukewarm water; to this add the milk and one pint of the flour to make sponge; set aside in a warm place to rise for one hour and twenty minutes, or until bubbles rise to the surface. When well risen, add the butter and sugar, thoroughly mixed; the salt, mace, eggs, well beaten, and remainder of flour (one and one-half pints), to make a soft dough; knead thoroughly, *but keep the dough soft.* Set in a warm place to rise again; should be light in one hour and a half. When light, roll out to about one-quarter inch in thickness on well floured kneading board and cut with doughnut cutter. Let rise again in a warm place, free from draft, for half an hour. Then drop into deep, boiling fat. Each doughnut should be turned frequently so as to brown evenly. The whole batch should be fried in about fifteen minutes. This makes three dozen. The entire process takes about four hours.

When through frying, peel and slice raw potato, remove the fat from the fire and drop the potato into it. When cool, not hard, remove potato and set fat away to harden. The potato prevents the fat from burning and will enable you to use it several times.

This recipe requires about two pounds of lard.

Doughnuts made by this method do no absorb the fat, to which many people object in the ordinary doughnuts.

It may require experience to make perfect bread, but any one can make perfect doughnuts by carefully following this recipe.

Early Fleischmann recipes offer a portrait of American cuisine. In this 1907 recipe, doughnuts are fried in two pounds of lard. Cincinnati sister company Proctor and Gamble introduced an all-vegetable shortening for deep-frying, which they called Crisco ® that would first appeal to Jewish consumers. (A)

ENGLISH BATH BUNS

2 cakes FLEISCHMANN'S YEAST   4 eggs
½ cup milk, scalded and cooled   4 cups sifted flour
1 tablespoonful sugar   ½ teaspoonful salt
¼ cup butter, melted   5 tablespoonfuls sugar

1 cup almonds, chopped

Dissolve yeast and one tablespoonful sugar in lukewarm milk. Add butter, eggs unbeaten, flour gradually, and the salt, beating thoroughly. This mixture should be thick, but not stiff enough to handle. Cover and let rise in warm place one and one-half hours, or until light. Sprinkle balance of sugar and almonds over top, mix very lightly and drop into well-greased muffin pans. Cover and let rise until light, which should be in about one-half hour. Bake fifteen to twenty minutes in a moderately hot oven. These buns should be rough in appearance.

Although Fleischmann's introduced cookbooks as far back as 1877, it wasn't until 1910 that the Company introduced its first give-away cookbook containing only yeast recipes. (A)

Responding to the urbanization of America, in 1919 Julius decided to move headquarters to New York City. His son and heir apparent Charles II had died in an aircraft accident at Long Beach the year before, and Julius felt the move would be best for all. Julius had hoped that his son Charles could have taken on some of the responsibility of running the company, but now he realized that he would have to continue to shoulder the burden. Cincinnati was sad to see the company headquarters and the prominent founding family depart for the financial capital of the country. Headquarters was established between the Hudson docks and Greenwich Village, at 701 Washington Street (shown here). 419 Plum Street in Cincinnati faded into secondary-market obscurity. (CL)

The "Eat More Bread" campaign launched in 1912 was promoted by a character called "John Dough," an obvious forerunner of the modern Pillsbury Dough Boy. During the "Eat More Bread" campaign the company gave away thousands of recipe books to train homemakers in the art of home baking. In a reversal of Marie Antoinette, another ad commands the parent, "Give them Bread!"—bread made from Fleischmann's yeast, of course. (A)

Fleischmann's established the marketing tool of wrapper premiums, awarding household items for the redemption of yeast labels. For 50 labels one could receive a silver spoon, for 300 a small carving set. (A)

FLEISCHMANN'S YEAST
FREE SILVERWARE FREE

We will give users of our Yeast in exchange for YEL-LOW LABELS AND TINFOIL WRAPPERS taken from it, at the rate specified, the articles mentioned in the following Premium List. **WE WILL NOT REDEEM LABELS AND WRAPPERS FROM OR THROUGH TRADING STAMP AGENCIES.**

PREMIUM LIST.

10 Labels . . .	One Handsome ALUMINUM THIMBLE		
25	Labels and Tin Foil Wrappers,	One Silver-Plated TEA SPOON	
50	"	"	TABLE SPOON
50	"	"	TABLE FORK
50	"	"	BUTTER KNIFE
50	"	"	SUGAR SPOON
50	"	"	PEPPER SHAKER
50	"	"	SALT SHAKER
75	"	"	TABLE KNIFE
75	"	"	PICKLE FORK
100	"	"	CREAM LADLE
125	"	"	COLD MEAT FORK
125	"	"	BERRY SPOON
150	"	"	{ CHILD'S SET { Knife, Fork and Spoon
300	"	"	SOUP LADLE
300	"	One Small CARVING SET	
450	"	One Large CARVING SET	

25 LABELS AND 30 CENTS IN POSTAGE STAMPS
ONE REVISED PRESIDENTIAL COOK BOOK.

The Silverware is EXTRA plated, of HANDSOME design, and will wear five years.

The Carving Sets consist of Two Pieces, Knife and Fork, are of high quality steel, with horn handles, and are first class in every respect.

These premiums, WITH THE EXCEPTION OF THE COOK BOOK, can be obtained from our office in this city, or through our representatives, by presenting the required number of Labels attached to Tinfoil Wrappers.

They will not be mailed under any circumstances.

When COOK BOOK is wanted, twenty-five Labels and 30 CENTS IN POSTAGE STAMPS must be sent to THE FLEISCHMANN CO., No. 419 to 429 Plum Street, Cincinnati, Ohio, and that work will be forwarded to you promptly by mail. IT WILL NOT be delivered through our office in this city, nor through your grocer.

Labels must be attached to original Tinfoil wrappers or they will not be accepted in exchange for premiums.

The Company doted on jingles and tracing books for children. The staggering array of trade cards, calendars, and booklets produced by Fleischmann forms a veritable archive of late-Victorian and Edwardian Americana. (A)

Fleischmann's was among the first major American companies to recognize the power of children to sway a consumer's buying decisions. (A)

"Is this it, miss?" "Yes, sir; that's the kind—Fleischmann's"

RECIPES

Bohemian Hoska

TO beaten egg, add sugar and butter creamed. Beat until light. Add milk which has been scalded and cooled, stir well, then add yeast which has been previously dissolved in lukewarm water, and two·cups of sifted flour, to make a thin batter. Beat until smooth. Cover and let rise until light—about one hour. Add almonds, citron and raisins well-floured, the rest of the flour, or enough to make a soft dough, and lastly, the salt. Knead well. Cover and set aside in warm place, free from draught, to rise until double in bulk—about one and one-half hours. Divide into three parts. Make three braids, place in well-greased pan, one on top of the other. Let rise thirty minutes. Brush with egg, diluted with water. Bake in moderate oven forty-five to fifty minutes. While hot, ice with plain frosting.

See recipe for plain frosting, page 31.

1 cake
FLEISCHMANN'S YEAST
¼ cup lukewarm water
2 cups milk, scalded and cooled
½ cup sugar
¼ cup citron cut fine
⅓ cup butter
1 egg
½ teaspoonful salt
½ cup raisins
½ cup almonds chopped

Only sweet dreams after a Bread-and-Milk supper.

Fifty years into the reorganization of American baking, Fleischmann's still gave homage to Charles' origins through this recipe of his countrymen. (A)

62

ENGLISH MUFFINS

1 cake FLEISCHMANN'S YEAST	2 tablespoonfuls sugar
1 cup milk, scalded and cooled	4 tablespoonfuls lard or butter, melted
1 cup lukewarm water	6 cups sifted flour
	1 teaspoonful salt

Dissolve yeast and sugar in lukewarm liquid, add lard or butter and three cups of flour. Beat until smooth, add rest of flour, or enough to make a soft dough, and the salt. Knead until smooth and elastic. Place in well-greased bowl, cover and set aside in warm place to rise. When double in bulk, which should be in about two hours, form with hand into twelve large, round biscuits. Cover and set aside for about one-half hour.

Then, with rolling-pin, roll to about one-fourth inch in thickness, keeping them round. Have ungreased griddle hot and bake ten minutes. Brown on both sides. As they brown, move to cooler part of stove, where they will bake more slowly, keeping them warm in the oven until all are baked. They can be reheated in this way or split and toasted on the griddle. These muffins are delicious served hot with plenty of butter.

This English muffin recipe from 1916 is a typical example of the kind of recipe popular at the time. While the American homemaker kept right on baking through World War I, by the 1920s the pioneering days of home baking were drawing to a close. America was becoming more urbanized, and one's God-given daily bread could be easily purchased at the local market or bakery. Home sales dipped precariously, some of which was made up by the increase in bakery sales. Prohibition in 1919 closed down the Fleischmann distilleries and breweries. Prior to this, alcohol accounted for almost half the sales.

With Prohibition eliminating entire Fleischmann divisions, the company in the early 1920s concentrated on a triple strategy to reclaim its profitability. First, Fleischmann's continued to develop a strong market for its one-pound yeast cakes, which were sold to commercial bakers. By 1937 this product alone brought in $20 million a year. Second, home baking was still heavily promoted through cookbooks, as in this unusual recipe for potato biscuits. Third, the Company turned to the medical field for aid. (A)

FLEISCHMANN'S

1 cake
FLEISCHMANN'S
YEAST
1 pint milk
1 quart flour
1 egg
1 tablespoonful granulated sugar
1 quart mashed potatoes
¼ teaspoonful salt
Butter (size of an egg)

Potato Biscuit

POTATO Biscuits that are light and tender, with a delicious melt-in-your-mouth goodness, are assured you if you follow these directions. These ingredients will make 45 Biscuits.

Bake and mash six large potatoes, enough to make one quart, place in bowl, add salt, sugar and butter. Take a cupful of the milk, heat till lukewarm, dissolve yeast cake in it, and add enough flour to make a sponge—about one cup. Set sponge aside in warm place, free from draught, to rise.

Bring balance of the milk to boiling point and then add it to bowl containing the potatoes, salt, sugar and butter.

When sponge has risen and dropped back, add it to bowl containing the other materials, also add the egg well beaten, remainder of flour and mix all together thoroughly.

Let rise in a warm place. Butter a baking sheet and drop the mixture from a tablespoon, as the dough should not be handled. Let rise again and bake from fifteen to twenty minutes.

Dr. Philip Hawk at Jefferson Medical College in Philadelphia was commissioned by Fleischmann's to study the curative health values of baker's yeast. Published in the Journal of the American Medical Association, his study concluded that the ingestion of yeast was useful in the treatment of boils, acne, and ailments of the gastro-intestinal tract. Fleischmann's reprinted the article and sent it out to the entire American medical community. Indeed, it seemed that Saccharomyces cerevisiae could be taken as a vitamin supplement for it is a rich source of B-compounds, including folic acid and niacin-- and it contains 50% protein. Still disappointed with sales after a short trial, the Company signed with the J. Walter Thompson advertising agency in 1920, which began to experiment

with the marketing of smaller foil-wrapped packets of yeast for home medicinal purposes. Using realistic testimonials, this highly successful tactic became an advertising legend. Advertising of medicinal yeast would transform Fleischmann's yeast from a leavening agent to a food itself, one to be eaten directly from the package as a health supplement. After all, the yeast was loaded with vitamin D and the B complex vitamins. Among the first ads were ones that suggest, "Yeast is replacing sallow complexions with the radiancy of healthy beauty. Yeast is the latest and best addition to milady's toilet table." (A)

Thousands of unsolicited letters arrived praising the health benefits of eating Fleischmann's yeast. These were first used in the campaign with models' photographs, then with photographs of the real endorsers. Fleischmann's began adding these testimonials to its cookbooks. Unfortunately, references to the treatment of constipation, acne, and migraine headaches appeared shortly after this recipe for a Currant Tea Ring. (A)

CURRANT TEA RING

2 cakes Fleischmann's Yeast	7 cups sifted flour
1 cup milk, scalded and cooled	6 tablespoonfuls shortening
1 cup lukewarm water	½ cup sugar
1 tablespoonful sugar	3 eggs
	½ teaspoonful salt

Simply delicious! This recipe makes two large or three small rings.

Dissolve yeast and one tablespoonful sugar in lukewarm liquid. Add three cups of flour and beat until smooth. Add shortening and sugar thoroughly creamed, and eggs, beaten until light, the remainder of the flour gradually, or enough to make a moderately soft dough, and the salt. Turn on board, knead lightly. Place in greased bowl. Cover and set aside in a warm place to rise, for about two hours.

Roll out in oblong piece, one-fourth-inch thick. Brush with melted butter. Sprinkle with brown sugar, currants and cinnamon. Roll up lengthwise and place in a circle on a large, shallow greased pan or baking sheet. With scissors cut three-fourths-inch slices, almost through. Turn each slice partly on its side, pointing away from center. This should give the effect of a many-pointed star and show the different layers with the filling.

Cover and let rise one hour, or until light, and bake twenty-five minutes. Just before putting in oven, glaze with egg, diluted with milk. Ice while hot with plain icing. (See recipe for icing on page 40.)

[44]

As America dug its heels deep into the Great Depression, Fleischmann's presented consumers images of domesticity perhaps more suited to Sands Point and Indian Hill than to the rank-and-file. (A)

says Prof. Dr.
FRANZ MÜLLER,
of Berlin,
the celebrated
pharmacologist

While the "Yeast for Health" campaign was one of the most expensive and profitable ad campaigns of all time, J. Walter Thompson soon realized that the consumption of yeast for well-being was part of the current vitamin fad—they had to assure sustainability through reinforcement and the authority of medical fact. The Thompson agency turned toward a vast pool of European doctors with impressive scowls and exotic names to further endorse their product. In 1928, a Miss Eaton on staff called 60 doctors and scientists in seven European countries and secured 19 testimonials. (A)

DR. BOSELLINI is a member of the Italian Royal Medical Academy and author of "Dermatology in its Relation to Internal Medicine."

"Bad Skin is usually Nature punishing you for internal neglect—"

declares
DR. PIETRO BOSELLINI
of Rome

THE doctor who makes the above statement is one of the most famous skin specialists in Italy. He is Dr. Pietro Bosellini, Professor of Dermatology in the University of Rome. *He states:—*

"Skin troubles as a rule must be attacked from *inside* the body. When waste matter collects and stagnates in the system, the blood absorbs poisons. The resistance of the skin to infection is weakened and . . . pimples, boils or blotches may appear."

To correct this unpleasant condition, Dr. Bosellini advises . . . *yeast!*

"Fresh yeast (he says) has remarkable power to . . . 'tone' the intestinal tract and restore regular evacuations. The effect on the health is often remarkable. Digestion improves; headaches cease; *skin troubles soon clear up.*"

At any grocery, and most restaurants and soda fountains, you can get *Fleischmann's* Yeast.* Just eat 3 cakes a day—before meals, or between meals and at bedtime—plain, or in water (about a third of a glass).

Then notice, after say 30 to 60 days, how much clearer your complexion has become.

Fleischmann's Yeast, you know, *stimulates* the intestines . . . softens the waste in the body so you can eliminate it easily. The result is, your system is cleansed. The poisons that were causing your bad skin, bad breath, headaches, etc., are cleared away.

Fleischmann's Yeast, also, is very ★ rich in health-giving vitamins B, G and D, you know. Why don't *you* start eating it—now?

Important

Fleischmann's Yeast for health comes only in the foil-wrapped cake with the yellow label. It's yeast in its fresh, effective form — the kind doctors advise. Write for booklet. Standard Brands Inc., Dept. Y-D-5, 691 Washington St., N.Y.C.

"Our faces were all broken out."

"My sister and I both had skin trouble," *writes* Miss Virginia Koons (at left) *of Miami Beach, Fla.,* "and we could not understand why. We were so embarrassed we dreaded appearing in public. To add to our troubles, boils appeared.

"A doctor had advised yeast for one of our friends . . . We tried it, and in a week noticed improvement. Fleischmann's Yeast entirely cleared up our skin troubles."

In using advertisements see page 6

Using the imposing prescriptions of stern European doctors as well as heart-rending testimonials from consumers, the Thompson agency began to tout its client's product as the world's most natural laxative and purifier. The logic was clear—Louis Pasteur and Charles Fleischmann were pioneers in the science of yeast culture—Europe had lead the way in microbiology research. (A)

Fleischmann's found an unexpected market in teenage identity crises. Eating three cakes a day was sure to clear your skin and relieve antisocial tendencies. (A)

It was discovered that endorsements were often paid for. Celebrities such as crooner Rudy Vallee, star of radio's "Fleischmann Hour," also made yeast endorsements. Although taken for granted today, such practices were marginally scandalous at the time. The "Fleischmann Hour," which ran from 1929 to 1939, became one of the country's most popular radio shows; it is remembered for introducing the jazz trumpet of Louis Armstrong to America. (A)

R*udy* V ALLEE *says* . . .
"PUT YOURSELF · ACROSS"

What has he that others envy?—this charming youth who thrills millions with his crooning voice so full of magnetism, pathos, life. Is it merely added energy, added physical "drive"?

"AREN'T WE EVER GOING OUT ANY MORE?"

Dark clouds began filling the horizon. Although in a questionnaire survey of 30,000 American doctors, nearly half said they had prescribed yeast at some time or another, the physician-touted "purification by yeast" treatment ultimately outraged many in the medical profession. There was a counter-argument that live yeast (dry yeast was still on the drawing board) actually consumed B-vitamins from the body while moving through the digestive tract. (A)

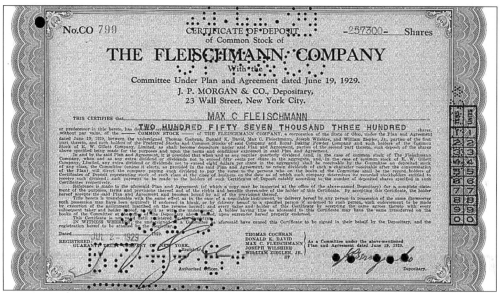

In June 1929, the Fleischmann Company absorbed Royal Baking Powder Company, E.W. Gillette Co., Widlar Food Products, and Chase & Sanborn to become Standard Brands. Fleischmann Company stock was exchanged for the Standard Brands issue, the transfers luckily made just before the Wall Street stock market crash in October. Max Fleischmann alone received $20,000,000 in the new stock. (A)

Chase and Sanborn Coffee — the freshest can of coffee you can buy!

Royal Puddings and Gelatins—for exciting flavors always reach for Royal.

Blue Bonnet—everything's better with Blue Bonnet on it.

Fleischmann's Margarine—it's made from 100% corn oil.

New Instant Chase and Sanborn with the pure coffee nectar.

Tender Leaf—the tea with more tea to it any way you brew it.

After the merger, the Fleischmann Division continued diversification into products such as margarine and vinegar. A Royal Gelatin plant was added to the Peekskill complex, a brand line from the Royal Baking Powder Company. By aerating vegetable oil in huge vats and chopping the mass into blocks, Fleischmann's Margarine was born. (A)

When Prohibition ended in 1933, Fleischmann's quietly fired up its stills at Peekskill, again producing gin and blended whiskey. After the 1929 creation of Standard Brands, members of the Fleischmann family continued to be visible at the new corporation and its successor companies. Max remained as chairman of Standard Brands until 1935, and then served as a director until his retirement in 1942. He stayed on as chair of the board's Finance Committee until his death in 1951. The hounds, hunting, and horses evoked by this ad well represents the lifestyle of both Max and his late brother Julius. (A)

The yeast packing line at the Fleischmann plant in Peekskill, New York is pictured here in 1938. With the creation of Standard Brands, the yeast company now served 60,000 bakeries, hotels, and restaurants, 300,000 grocers, with a fleet of 3,000 vehicles. Throughout the Depression, the company continued to use a variety of innovative approaches to keep its brand name fresh as home baking again increased. The Company took part in the 1934 and 1939 Worlds Fairs, having learned its lessons well at the Philadelphia Centennial Exposition. Perhaps these women could stay peppy by eating some of the product. (P)

Seven

THE THIRD GENERATION

Charles' brothers Louis and Max stayed in New York from the late 1870s on, where the elder Max ran eastern operations. Borrowing the idea from the phenomenally success concession at the Philadelphia Centennial Exposition of 1876, Max and Charles established the "Garden Fleischmann's Vienna Café and Restaurant" in the City, with Louis as manager in 1876. It was in business until 1904, and made Louis a millionaire. His philanthropy was legendary. Louis established the first bread line in America, which gave away day-old bread to the hungry.

RAOUL FLEISCHMANN

Louis' son Raoul Fleischmann graduated from Williams College in 1906. He worked for a time at his father's restaurant, and then ran the Fleischmann Vehicle Company that built and maintained the large fleet of Fleischmann delivery trucks. He operated the gigantic Bond Baking Company in New York City, located at 81st and East End Avenue in New York City. Although on a cadet branch of the clan, Raoul was also fabulously wealthy. Their New York apartment had five live-in servants plus three more full-time employees just to run the household. His stepson Gardner Botsford writes of a typical Fleischmann irony during Prohibition: Raoul, an heir to one of the world's greatest distillery fortunes, kept the liquor flowing for his entertaining needs. "Whenever our bootlegger went dry, he would make his own—not in a bathtub, as was commonly done, but in one of Nellie's (the laundress) wash boilers." No one could argue that this wasn't authentic "Fleischmann Gin." Raoul and his family acquired a summer home at Port Washington (Sands Point) on Long Island, the Hyannis Port of the Fleischmann clan after the Catskills lost its bloom. Raoul and his wife Ruth Gardner had many friends, from Harpo Marx to Averell Harriman.

In 1924 Raoul partnered with editor Harold Ross, investing an initial $25,000 to support publication of Ross' new comedy magazine centered on New York life. Over the next three years Fleischmann invested another $700,000 to insure the success of the fledgling periodical, and left the bread world far behind. Working with Ross, they became part of the effervescent, elite world of writers and poets, editors and publishers that met in the Round Table at the Hotel Algonquin, under the observing eye of Dorothy Parker. Raoul Fleischmann spent the rest of his life as publisher, president, chairman of the periodical, while Ross became its permanent editor. They formed a legendary Tom and Jerry of the periodical world, hating and respecting each other throughout. Raoul was succeeded by his son Peter Fleischmann in 1969, who maintained for years the editorial autonomy and unique style of this now immensely popular journal. Raoul's stepson Gardner Botsford became its editor. The magazine is The New Yorker. Raoul died in May 1969 at the age of 83, having provided yet another American icon from

Fleischmann family.

The third generation of American Fleischmann's developed generally independent of the patriarch Charles, and few were directly involved in Company operations for any great length of time. Still, most of the third generation shared their grandfather's passion for yachting, music, gardens, horses, art, and collecting mansions. Two of the grandsons stand out as truly amazing innovators in their own right.

JULIUS FLEISCHMANN, JR.

Julius Fleischmann Jr. was the eldest son of Julius Sr. and his first wife Lily. Whereas the senior Fleischmanns, Max, Julius Sr., and Bettie, were highly spirited, even flamboyant, Junior was reserved. But he developed similar passions for travel, polo, and yachting. Julius Jr. followed the nickname of his brother Charles at Hotchkiss School, Julius becoming "Little Junkie" on his own matriculation. Although active in the family business, he also was a publisher, owned several hotels, a theatrical production, and was president of the Ballet Russe of Monte Carlo. Julius Jr. became a serious student of cultural anthropology. Using his four yachts, all named Camargo, he sailed the oceans looking for lost tribes and reporting on the colorful diversity of human life around the globe. He shared this particular passion for ocean travel and distant vistas with Uncle Max and his cousin Christian Holmes II. Junkie's haunts included the Cocos Islands, New Hebrides (Vanuatu), Solomon Islands, New Guinea, Sri Lanka, and the Arabian Peninsula. His journals of his trips to Melanesia during the 1930s chronicle the rapidly changing cultures. He collected Melanesian artifacts, which were donated to the Cincinnati Natural History Museum, another great 'family' project. He was also an avid shell collector, as was his cousin Christian Holmes II.

Junkie is perhaps best known for helping to establish the resort town of Naples, Florida. Shortly after a visit in 1946, Junkie began purchasing lots in and around the city. In 1952, he established the Neapolitan Enterprises for his development interests. There he purchased a commercial building and renamed it the Beach Patio, and built a fashion salon—all in Old Naples along Third Street. In 1962 he constructed Fleischmann Central, a two-story building of shops and offices. Several other building followed, including the Swan Court, the Seminole Market, and the Antique Addict filled with the artifacts and antiques from his trips around the world.

At Naples, Junkie Fleischmann restored Nehrling's famous botanical gardens, and installed a special glass house for his collection of orchids. He cleared a trail through an overgrowth that had built up since the garden's establishment in 1917. Dr. Nehrling has been an ornithologist and was fascinated with tropical plants. He developed many hybrids on his 30-acre gardens. Fleischmann removed the debris, nurtured old plants, dug ponds, and planted thousands of new growths. He added a flock of tropical birds to the newly restored botanical park, which he named Caribbean Gardens. Junkie hired Joel Kuperberg, a graduate student in botany, to manage the gardens. The two traveled the world collecting exotic species of plants and birds for the park. Occasionally a swan or flamingo would escape and often end up as dinner for the neighboring alligators. Again, cousin Christian Holmes also loved orchids, tropical fish, and exotic birds, and raised them in profusion on his private Coconut Island that he had entirely transformed in Hawai`i.

Dorette Fleischmann was a delegate to the Atlantic Treaty Association and a member of the Atlantic Council. A graceful and elegant woman, Mrs. Fleischmann was on the best-dressed list in the 1930s. She had a wide circle of friends in the entertainment world. She donated much of her dress collection to the Cincinnati Art Museum towards the end of her life, which occurred in March 1994. Junkie and Dorette had three children: Charles Fleischmann III, Dorette Louise Fleischmann, and Joan Fleischmann Tobin.

CHRISTIAN R. HOLMES II

Christian Rasmus Holmes II, the creator of the tropical fantasy of Coconut Island in Hawai`i, the real "Gilligan's Island," was raised in an environment of extraordinary personal achievement—he lived up to that tradition and perhaps exceeded them all. His creation of a Hawaiian paradise from an eleven-acre rock in Kane`ohe Bay makes Holmes' estate by far the most exotic of the Fleischmanns' many mansions, a 'Fleischmann Rococo.'

Christian was born in 1899 to great wealth that had been accumulated through the innovations and business savvy of his mother Bettie's family and especially of her father Charles Fleischmann. Christian's father, Dr. Christian R. Holmes, was one of the outstanding men in American medicine. Not much is known of the early life of Christian II, although the photographs of a rather perturbed little boy of five, shown previously, dressed in skirts with his brother Carl and parents, speak much to his character. His father recalled in a letter to his son on the Western Front, "The other day in our garden, I happened to glance at the weather vane over the stable and it brought sad thoughts to me; at the same time, I could not help smiling because the old horse is certainly full of holes which you put there as a boy when you first got your .22 rifle."

Christian spent a portion of his post-World War I youth in New York while working at the Fleischmann Company. Here he married his first wife in 1922, Albertine Osborne Peck of New England, who had briefly been a stage actress. They had two sons, Christian Holmes III (1923-1999?) and William Dayton Holmes (1926-2000).

Christian and his family moved to Santa Barbara in 1924, the year that his grandmother Henriette passed away and his mother was finishing up matters in Cincinnati prior to her move to New York. Christian may have been encouraged to move West by his uncle Max and his aunt Sarah, who had relocated to California in 1919 to command the U.S. Army Balloon School at Arcadia.

Christian Holmes had a reputation as an athlete, aesthete, and an eccentric—a fun-loving man with nearly unlimited resources. While his uncle Julius may have been the Great Gatsby, Christian was more an Errol Flynn (who became his close friend). The same sort of frontier impetus that drove Charles Fleischmann to the American Midwest drove Christian Holmes across the Pacific to Hawai`i. After the War, Holmes was restless and not content to be a Fleischmann executive any more than his Uncle Max. Both nephew and uncle put great emphasis on adventure and travel in their lives—making an impact, being monumental.

During the California years, Christian Holmes, like his mother and cousin Junkie, traveled extensively to collect artifacts. Like Julius Jr. and unlike his uncle Max who collected trophy heads, Chris brought back botanical specimens, and live animals from around the world. His excursions often took him to Hawai`i, where he was awestruck by its beauty. Its escapist images resonated deeply with Holmes, as it did with countless other Americans and Europeans with dreams of tropical paradise and rejuvenation. To create a new life in a new world, Christian undoubtedly had much in common with his grandfather Charles Fleischmann. Christian moved to the Hawaiian Islands in 1933.

Raoul Fleischmann, publisher of the New Yorker, is pictured here in 1939. (OM)

Julius Jr. married Dorette Kruse on January 9, 1928 in Christ Church in Cincinnati. Mrs. Fleischmann attended Miss Doherty's School and Smith College. They had three children, Charles III ("Skip"), Dorette, and Joan. (OM)

With two of his small children, Julius Fleischmann Jr. traveled around the world on his 225-foot yacht, Camargo 1, carrying the flag of the New York Yacht Club. The journey was chronicled in Footsteps in the Sea and of course many of the artifacts collected on the trip ended up in the Cincinnati Museum of Natural History. Their mapping of the islands and sea lanes of the South pacific to survey plants for the U.S. Department of Agriculture were used by the U.S. military during World War II. Junkie maintained homes in Cincinnati, New York, and Naples, Florida. Mr. and Mrs. Fleischmann summered in Cape Cod, and wintered in Naples. Junkie inherited Winding Hill from his father, and the Camargo Hunt tradition. (M)

Junkie Fleischmann supported the New York Public Library, Metropolitan Opera, the Ballet Russe de Monte Carlo, the Congress for Cultural Freedom, UNESCO, the Bilderberg Conferences, and the Council on Foreign Affairs. Junkie was, in fact, president of the Ballet Russe de Monte Carlo. He also produced a dozen or so plays for the Broadway stage. For his outstanding cultural contributions, Junkie became a chevalier of the French Legion of Honor. Julius Fleischmann Jr. passed away in 1968. (CF)

From his father's old suite atop the Art Deco Carew Tower, Cincinnati's tallest building, Charles III carries the family torch and runs the Fleischmann Foundation. He is a generous supporter of the Cincinnati Art Museum, Cincinnati Museum Center, and other cultural associations.

A handsome youth, Christian Holmes II attended Culver Military Academy in Ohio and was on its varsity football team. Although he may have spent some time at Yale, he appears to have graduated from Culver in 1917 and received an officer's commission just in time for World War I. All worried about young Christian, who spent most of the war in France and was usually negligent in writing home. (AH)

Christian became a hero—he was fearless on the battlefront, the "nerviest pup on the western front" wrote one commentator. He served with Theodore Roosevelt Jr. (left). For his bravery, he received the French Croix de Guerre and the Distinguished Service Award from the United States military. Christian did feel close to his family, though, eventually writing, "I feel a bit tired but my health is fine and the only thing I really want or need is to see my dear ones once again." Christian was shipped home in September 1918, and was discharged as a captain in February 1919. (B)

In Santa Barbara, Holmes (center) established the Feather Hill Ranch to raise poultry. Here he installed the largest private zoo in the United States. Among the animals at the menagerie were bears and an elephant. He also built Linden Lodge as a hideaway in the nearby mountains at San Marcos Pass. This house burned down in 1939 or 1940. Later, when Holmes closed the Feather Hill Ranch, he donated 142 pet birds to the aviary established at Kapi`olani Park on O`ahu. This collection was eventually incorporated into the Honolulu Zoo. That Holmes loved animals was the source of many vivid remembrances: Christian once kept a suite at the St. Francis Hotel in San Francisco—fairly ordinary except for the snakes he kept as roommates. Every now and then the serpents would get loose and cause an uproar. Since the reptiles were inclined to climb and move up the stairwells, the hotel management finally made Holmes take over the entire top floor. (AH).

In California, Holmes was divorced from Albertine Peck and married the beautiful Katherine MacDonald (pictured here and on the next page), a Hollywood actress known as the "American Beauty" in 1928. MacDonald's career began with silent films in the late 1910s and continued to 1925. The epitome of style and grace of her times, she had a popular following and was promoted by B.P. Schulberg, one of the originators of United Artists. She also worked on silent films produced by First National. Christian and his new wife were one of Hollywood's beautiful couples. They had one daughter, Ann (b. 1930). Holmes and MacDonald ended their marriage in 1932. Mother and baby Ann stayed behind in Santa Barbara, establishing a home on Hot Springs Road. (B) (B)

On O'ahu, Holmes purchased the estate of farm equipment king C.F. Case Deering in Waikiki from Deering's widow, Mary. The mansion was opposite languid Kapi'olani Park at 2709 Kalakaua Avenue. The fabulous, three-story masterpiece of whitewashed stucco that Christian Holmes purchased in Waikiki was later named "Queen's Surf" after the beach house of Queen Lili'uokalani that once stood nearby. (AH)

The elegant Arts & Crafts-style mansion was designed by Chicago architects Holabird and Roche and built in 1916. Holmes paid $76,000 for the estate. The house, which stood about 100 feet back from the beach, had a tall central portion containing bedrooms and a lanai on the second floor, and an informal, Hawaiian-style penthouse on the third floor. One-story wings flanked both sides of the center portion of the house. The west wing contained a suite of two rooms and bath for Holmes. The east wing contained a dining room and kitchen. Bungalows for guests, servants' quarters, and other outbuildings completed the estate, which enclosed more than 100,000 square feet of prime Waikiki real estate. It took 18 servants to staff Queen's Surf. Following the tradition he had started at his ranch in Santa Barbara, Christian Holmes was soon throwing lavish parties, often large lu`au, for his friends at his Waikiki mansion. It remained his principal residence even after he created the Coconut Island retreat to his specifications. (AH)

In November 1933, Christian Holmes II subleased the island of Moku o Lo`e in Kane`ohe Bay, O`ahu, from Heeia Company for $1,000 per year. He had visited the island prior to leasing it, finding it deserted and covered in dense guava and lantana. With the Fleischmann millions, Holmes immediately set out to transform the weed-covered rock to a garden of tropical delights, renamed Coconut Island. He first extended a 42-inch cast iron pipe between the tiny island and O`ahu. Pure drinking water was piped here from the Ko`olau Range through several cisterns in the nearby hills. In 1934, a submarine telephone cable was established between mainland O`ahu and Coconut Island. In 1937, after clearing title with the Bishop Estate, he purchased the island outright. He invested over $1 million in its development with the addition of vast amounts of landfill and numerous landscaping and building improvements. (CH)

While the first coconut palms were planted by Charles and Bernice Pauahi Bishop around 1883, much of the extensive grove of coconut trees now seen on the island were established by Holmes—brought in by the barge load, as were all the exotic plants and flowering trees. (CH)

By August 1934, most of the island's structures had been built on the original core. Intentionally modest, the structures were designed for informal relaxation. (CH)

By far the most elaborate Holmes modification to Coconut Island would be the addition of 16 acres to the isle's total area. Much of the fill was sand poured directly on top of the reef platform encircling the natural rock island. The sand was removed from a feature appropriately known as Sand Island in Kane`ohe Bay, owned by the U.S. government. In addition to building beaches and lagoons, sand mixed with cement created walls for fishponds and swimming pools. Holmes owned hoppers and cement mixers for this operation. Channels for ships and boats were carved into the living reef surrounding Coconut Island. During the height of construction, Holmes had more than 200 workmen and 30 laundry women. Although the higher elevations of the island had a certain amount of soil, rich volcanic topsoil was obtained from local Japanese gardeners and added to the accreting Coconut Island. A concrete wall was built completely around the island, a project that took about three years to complete. (CH)

A view of Mokapu to the northeast from Coconut Island. Mokapu is home to the Kane`ohe Marine Corps Air Station. (A)

The local Hawaiian Tuna Packers had long maintained a cannery in Honolulu and a fishing station at Coconut Island. In fact, the owner lived on the islet in the 1920s and raised his family. In 1935, Bettie Holmes bought the Hawaiian Tuna Packers firm for her son to "keep him occupied." With Hawaiian Tuna Packers, Holmes would thrive. He applied the Fleischmann touch by creating and maintaining strong brand name identity. (TB)

Originally Holmes just owned the small fishing concern of Coral Gardens in Kane`ohe, with three sampans and twelve net fishermen in his employ. The operation was limited to the catch of turtles and sharks. However, when he saw how tuna was caught locally with minnows by Hawaiian Tuna Packers fishermen, he was fascinated. (FH) (FH)

Hawaiian Packers had no fishing boats of its own, but Holmes privately maintained one of the largest tuna boats in the territory, the Yamato Maru, which contributed substantially to the operation of the harvest. A smaller fishing boat, the Mona H, was also used. As Bettie had hoped, Holmes took an avid interest in the operations of Hawaiian Tuna Packers, a part of his long-term fascination with the study of marine biology. (LZ) (LZ)

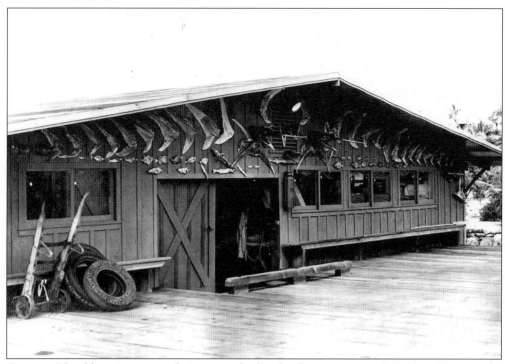

Coconut Island became a secondary service facility for the company and Holmes maintained a net house and a marine railway for minor repairs on-island. He kept a magnificent shell collection in the net house, an interest he shared with his cousin Junkie Fleischmann. (LZ)

The net house and two fish ponds are pictured here with He`eia and mainland O`ahu in the background. (A)

Three lagoons or mooring areas were built on the southwestern side of the island to accommodate larger ships. The ancient schooner Seth Parker was placed in one of these slips. This region also contained a shark pond and a larger fishpond. A dry dock, complete with marine railway, was installed here, as well as shops for carpentry, mechanics, and general boat repair. Just to the north of this region two jetties were extended out onto the reef, facing the He`eia shoreline. Four separate fishponds were constructed here. The net house was built on the western point of one of the jetties. Among the more ambitious enterprises at Coconut Island was the construction of a barrier shoal to protect the eastern side of the island, the region exposed to the open sea beyond the reefs. This shoal had two boat-turning basins, excavated into the coral, with a single outlet to the south. (CH)

On the north end of the island, a natural, saltwater swimming pool was established by enclosing a portion of the shoreline with rock and sand fill and excavating another portion into the base rock of the island. This created a shallow lagoon. The large swimming pool opened to the bay in two places. The filled portions of the lagoon, containing out buildings, were attached to Coconut Island by bridges. Holmes procured from the U.S. Navy two giant searchlights to help illuminate the pool for nighttime swimming. The pool was also graced with water slides and a shower house. A beach house for guests was built adjacent to the pool. (PF)

Holmes built a road completely encircling the island, much of which was lined with beautiful trees and exotic plants that went wild in the tropical setting. Other gardens supported rare cacti and other succulents. Along the west coast of the island, Holmes constructed several servants' quarters, a hothouse for his orchids, and a fernery. Nearer the shore he had several aquaria installed for his tropical fish collection, and he raised shrimp in tanks for his own consumption. Clam and oyster beds were established near the shoreline on the west and south portions of the island. Holmes also raised eels. A pumphouse to bring seawater to the marine aquaria was set in the center of the island on the western shoreline. Adjacent buildings were used for storage and refrigeration. (GN)

The shark pond near the Seth Parker was a commercial enterprise. A dyed-in-the-wool Fleischmann, Holmes sold shark liver oil as a vitamin supplement in San Francisco and shark fin as a delicacy to chefs in Honolulu's Chinatown. This photo was shot in a shark pond operated by the Hawai`i Institute of Marine Biology on the island. (A)

One wonders if this Great White, caught by Holmes and his crew, also ended up as noodle soup in Honolulu restaurants. (BS)

As built by Holmes, the main house of Coconut Island was a fairly simple, straightforward ranch house. Constructed of hollow tile, the home consisted of an office and kitchen in the north wing, a large dining and living room in the center, a patio-lanai, and four bedrooms and bath in the south wing. The house was erected around a lattice-covered central fountain and garden area hung with baskets of ferns. Orchids in pots were set out along the patio walls. The courtyard walls contained 10 built-in aquaria filled with Holmes' exotic fish. There were six glass aquaria in the main house. (AH)

The study in the main house was furnished with antique Spanish furniture. (AH)

(*above*) The lawn of the main house is pictured here in the 1990s. The huge lanai of the main house was furnished in Hawaiian style with lauhala mats and bamboo-covered walls that opened onto a lawn that afforded a spectacular view of the sea and Mokapu Peninsula. The lawn contained artfully arrayed lily ponds filled with ornamental carp and ducks. (A)

(*left*) Mona Kekahakulani Hind, here with one of the island's chimpanzees, became Christian Holmes II's third wife at a ceremony officiated by Judge Judd in Honolulu on April 17, s1935. Of the famous Parker family of the Big Island, Mona Hind was a direct descendent of King Kamehameha I. (FH)

One of the more lively funhouses Holmes built on the island was a long hall located on the north side of the island. It contained a two-lane, manual pin bowling alley and was furnished with rattan chairs. One could also play pool or ping pong, get a soda from the Coke machine, or try one's luck with the slot machines (Bettie preferred bowling). From the ceiling hung a superb model airplane collection. Holmes also built a shooting gallery, a direct descendent of his mother's playhouse in Sands Point. While Holmes was visiting the Playland shoreline amusement park in San Francisco, he came upon a shooting gallery. He bought it from the owner and shipped it intact to Honolulu. One of Holmes' servants remembered, "When you flipped on the switches, everything would turn on. There was a player piano that played, and the ducks would be flying and swimming on a pond, and the rabbits would be hopping. . . the ducks would actually swim on real water." He also kept a player piano in the gallery. The larger recreation hall housed Holmes' extensive collection of artifacts and knickknacks from around the world. These included, according to one observer, "mummified Indian heads, hunting knives and guns of every description, mounted birds and giant lizards, bear rug trophies, shark heads, and grotesquely carved primitive figures." Holmes possessed a jeweled Venetian dagger with the monogram "NB" that was believed to have belonged to Napoleon I. (AH)

Holmes and his new wife did not live in the main house, however, but in a simple cottage known as the Retreat. Located up the hill and about 40 feet to the south of the main house, the Retreat was a cozy place to get away from the endless stream of visitors Chris and Mona Holmes were fond of entertaining. The cottage contained a large living room with a high ceiling, a capacious bathroom, a comfortable bedroom, and a small but deep private swimming pool surrounded by walls of orchids. The house was staffed with its own maid. (A)

Somewhat of a Gatsby himself like his uncle Julius, Christian Holmes roared back and forth between his Waikiki mansion and his private island in this elongated Packard, driven by Jimmy Teshima. On the summit of the hill just south of the retreat cottage, Holmes built an observation lounge, another feature of Holmes' remarkable lifestyle. The hexagonal building with large picture windows (see the aerial shot shown previously) provided a spectacular view of Kane`ohe Bay and the Ko`olau Range. The interior of the lounge was arrayed with couch sections along the walls and a bar off to one side. A dictaphone/telephone line linked the observatory with the kitchen so snacks and drinks could be ordered. On top of the observatory was a tower and searchlight and, nearby, a red beacon—reminding visitors and planes that this spot was just south of the glide path of the Marine Air Base main runway at Mokapu. (LZ)

Junior Lee (left) and Jack Kim pose with two of Holmes' three chimpanzees. The chimpanzees were the life of the party—often one of the apes would be dressed in white tie and tails and seated next to an unescorted lady guest. Another would mimic Mrs. Holmes on the phone. Sometimes the primates were sent in to awaken guests in the morning. Holmes established a rather fabulous zoo at his island paradise. A kennel for about fifteen dogs was built on the island, complete with a dog food kitchen and dog bath. One report mentions a zebra, another saw a camel. A talented mynah reportedly sang "Isle of Capri" to amazed guests. Holmes brought over tigers, a giraffe, and "all kinds of monkeys." Among the various birds imported to the island, exotic peacocks and pheasants are vividly remembered. Holmes had a beautiful butterfly collection housed under glass in a room to itself. By a circuitous path of association, Holmes thus provided the nucleus for two Hawaiian institutions: the Honolulu Zoo and Hawai`i Institute of Marine Biology, similarly to what Julius, Junkie, and Max Fleischmann had done in their communities. (LZ)

In 1938, Christian Holmes outdid his relatives and ordered a baby elephant for his private zoo. A two-year-old, 1,400-pound female Indian elephant from Hagenbeck Zoo in Germany, was brought through San Francisco and transferred to a freighter for final shipment to Hawai`i. The pachyderm, named Beckel, was given a large, stone-walled pen all to herself next to the monkey cage, under the care of Junior Lee. Holmes became very fond of the animal, who learned to pick up the flamboyant Fleischmann heir with his trunk. (LZ)

Not to be used for surfing—Holmes ordered a Chris Craft, mid-engine, front and rear cockpit speedboat, which was a very sleek machine, with varnished mahogany and white lines between boards. It was basically built for high-speed operation on lakes and flat water. Holmes took delivery in Honolulu and piloted over to Coconut Island. When the weather kicked up and the great breakers rolled in, the only way to keep on course was to go full speed. Inevitably the motor broke through the floorboards and went right through the bottom of the boat right off Mokapu. As the boat sank, the occupants swam to shore without event. Holmes put in a claim to his insurance agent, and received an identical boat. The new vessel, appropriately called the Auwe (H. "lamentation"), survived for a time, then was destroyed when the throttle was floored in reverse, causing the boat to crash upon the dock, break apart, and sink. No claim was submitted that time around. The Auwe, piloted by Captain Iguchi, is seen here in happier moments. (LZ)

George Putnam (left), his wife Amelia Earhart, and copilot Paul Mantz (center) at Queen's Surf. With nearly unlimited wealth and his Hollywood network from his days at Santa Barbara with Katherine MacDonald, Christian Holmes now had perhaps the world's most spectacular island setting on which a glittering social life of parties, retreats, and festive celebrations could be held. The international "propeller" set of the late 1930s was incandescent. It was the streamlined era of Wallis Simpson and the Duke of Windsor, of a young Howard Hughes, and of King Carol II of Romania and his mistress Magda Lupescu. Amelia Earhart and crew were houseguests at both Queen's Surf and Coconut Island in 1935; she left a broken propeller as a memento of her stay. (BPBM)

A rare shot of Christian Holmes (center, with polka-dotted robe) entertaining his guests, most notably Amelia Earhart and George Putnam (left), in the living room of Queen's Surf. (BS)

Shirley Temple was thrown a birthday party at the Waikiki estate around 1935. At this fête, all the children were given two live rabbits to take home. (BPBM)

Bettie Fleischmann Holmes was a peripatetic visitor at her son's estates at Queen's Surf and Coconut Island. Arriving with her daughter-in-law Mrs. Carl Holmes (left) on the Lurline, Bettie is greeted by Olympic surfing legend Duke Kahanamoku and Mona Hind. Duke became a life-long friend of Christian's. (CH)

Bettie dining at the Queen's Surf estate. Hawaiian luaus were the most popular form of entertainment in the Holmes' island paradise. (FH)

Holmes' co-prankster Errol Flynn. A Coconut Island carpenter recalled the big parties on the island: "we . . . would watch the people, about 200 or 300 of them, all guests coming from Mokapu base." Holmes brought a Hawaiian orchestra out to the island about three times a week, complete with singers and dancers. Holmes rarely got to bed before 5:00 A.M. According to another guest: "Once in a while there would be about ten people at the table for some dinner or something. But [at times] they were bigger than that like when you had Bing Crosby and all these other people that came from Los Angeles and New York. . . . The [meals] were all very informal, just a buffet type meal, always very casual, very friendly, it was a relaxed sort of feeling that you got there. He wanted you to just come and enjoy the place like he did. He was a very nice host." Guests remember Alice Faye visiting Coconut Island, as well as prizefighter Jack Demsey. Johnny "Tarzan" Weismueller, John Wayne, Bette Davis, Samuel Goldwyn, Hal Roach, Noël Coward, Spencer Tracy, and Janet Gaynor all were entertained on Coconut Island. Holmes was friends with the Rockefellers, Herbert Hoover, William Randolph Hearst Jr., Averell Harriman, and tobacco heiress Doris Duke. (A)

The landmark that would be most remembered by visitors to Coconut Island is the moored sailing ship Seth Parker. Holmes purchased the old schooner in 1935 from radio personality Phillips Lord. Lord's character was a New England parson named Seth Parker. Lord sailed from New York, calling at various ports to broadcast his weekly show on the ship's own shortwave station, KRNA. The Frigidaire Company underwrote the trip, demonstrating the reliability of their refrigerators and air conditioners on this trip around the world. Initially the voyage was a great success, but in February 1935, the Seth Parker promptly sailed into a typhoon off the coast of American Samoa. The ship barely survived, and the radio show was cancelled. Holmes bought the 188-ft. schooner for $10,000, filled it with sardines, and sent it back to Honolulu. It (and the sardines) survived the trip, but because of the general lack of seaworthiness of the schooner, it was towed to an artificial lagoon at Coconut Island and scuttled in a few feet of water. (FH)

Holmes modified the Seth Parker's interior to use as a motion picture theater, laboratory, and bar. Guests could sunbathe on the deck. A few staterooms were equipped for overnight stay. Reflecting his avid interest in marine biology, Holmes installed laboratories in the stern of the schooner to serve Hawaiian Tuna Packers fisheries research. Although Holmes finally found a ship large enough to compete with the Fleischmann's legacies of the Hiawathas, Camargos, and Haidas, the Seth slowed rotted away—today all that is left is a mound of green vegetation where the proud Seth Parker once was berthed. (AH)

Holmes' sons by Albertine Peck, Christian III, and William Dayton (left and right of Duke Kahanamoku), were frequent visitors to the island, as were Mona's daughter, Lamie Lucas, and son, Charlie Lucas, by a previous marriage. (BS)

The long party continued until September 1941, when Bettie Fleischmann Holmes passed away in New York. While Christian and Mona were absent to attend to his mother's affairs, Coconut Island was strafed by planes of the Imperial Japanese Airforce—December 7, 1941. The island was located only a few hundred meters from the threshold of the main runway at Kane`ohe Marine Corps Air Base, which was largely destroyed. The next day, Holmes' valuables were packed up and taken away—most of the island's personnel, many of Japanese American descent, were told to leave Holmes' property by the U.S. government. (USAF)

Ann Holmes, Christian Holmes' daughter by Katherine MacDonald, also visited. Holmes allowed children to play in the Retreat House, with its gigantic tiled bathroom. Chris would hose down the floor to let the youngsters run and slide. The room was adjacent to the outdoor Orchid Swimming Pool. On one occasion, he stocked the pool with Conger eels, floated in a few hundred-dollar bills and dared anyone to jump in to retrieve them. (AH)

Holmes returned to Coconut Island the following summer, but the great parties and carefree life in the islands were over. Like his family during WWI, Holmes donated his Queen's Surf estate to the war effort for the duration. He sent his collection of tropical fish to the Steinhart Aquarium in San Francisco. Then his health began to degenerate. In late December 1943, he was sent to New York for medical care. The next month Mona divorced Holmes. In February, while undergoing treatment for depression, Holmes was found dead. He was only 47 years old. Chris Holmes' ashes were brought to Hawai`i and scattered in Kane`ohe Bay by Alan Davis and the skippers of Hawaiian Tuna Packers. Most of the Holmes' personal effects, his great art works and furniture, were sold at auction. Holmes' menagerie of birds and mammals, including the elephant and chimps, became the nucleus of the new Honolulu Zoo. (FH)

(inset) President Franklin D. Roosevelt, just after his unprecedented fourth-term nomination, stayed at the Queen's Surf estate in Waikiki in the summer of 1944 for a mid-war meeting with his generals. On July 27, Roosevelt dined with General Douglas MacArthur and admirals Nimitz, Leahy, and Halsey at the Holmes mansion. The next day the President threw a lawn party, which included a Hawaiian orchestra, a vocalist, and a hula dancer. Newspaper articles at the time painted the scene of an ebullient, effusive Roosevelt suavely rebuking his vain Pacific commander. In truth, Roosevelt was dying. During the War, bunk beds were installed upstairs at Queen's Surf to provide sleeping arrangements for about 30 servicemen. A "charming Honolulu matron" and her husband were installed in one of the guest cottages to look after the naval pilots and their friends. Soon after the war ended, the military gave up its interest in the Queen's Surf property. The estate was sold, then transformed into a nightclub by Spencer Weaver. Sterling Mossman was hired as the lead entertainer at the club. The buildings and grounds of the old estate were demolished in 1971 for an expansion of Kapi`olani Park and beach. Where Holmes entertained Shirley Temple and Amelia Earhart, and Roosevelt had dined with MacArthur, a snack bar now served teriyaki plate lunches to the public. (USAF)

On 15 January 1945, Alan Davis of the Hawaiian Trust Company, executor for Holmes' estate, leased Coconut Island to the U.S. government. Coconut Island became a recreation center for the U.S. military. Like in the heyday of Christian Holmes, parties with up to 200 individuals were held on the island. Navy boats brought the guests over from mainland Oʻahu. Over a section of the swimming pool, the Army built a dance pavilion. Holmes' shooting gallery, shipped board by board from San Francisco, was a popular attraction for the young men and their guests. (USAF)

Fleischmann's®

ACTIVE DRY

Yeast®

RECIPE ON BACK

NET WT. 1/4 OZ (7g)

During the War, the Peekskill plant began to mass-produce an active dry yeast. It had previously experimented with dried yeast for animal feed. A breakthrough in research in the 1930s allowed dormant, dried yeast to be transported long distances without refrigeration. When reconstituted, the yeast would spring back to life and could be used like the original compressed cakes. It was ideal to help feed service personnel overseas—so much so that in 1943 the U.S. government awarded a coveted Army and Navy "E" designation to Fleischmann's. The company went on to win two more stars for excellence before the war was over. For many years, both active dry yeast and yeast cakes were available in the market. (A)

Eight

STANDARD BRANDS
ENTERS WORLD WAR II

As Joe knows, the end of the Depression and the entry into World War II was also a time of continued scientific innovation for Fleischmann's Division of Standard Brands. It was discovered that vitamin B1 was a cure for beriberi. Scientists at the company worked feverishly to improve strains of yeast that produced B1. When it was developed in 1940 and accepted by the American Medical Association, it allowed the company to promote enriched bread. (A)

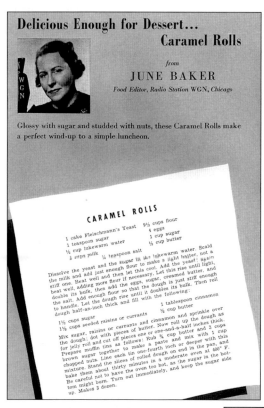

Delicious Enough for Dessert...
Caramel Rolls

from

JUNE BAKER

Food Editor, Radio Station WGN, Chicago

Glossy with sugar and studded with nuts, these Caramel Rolls make a perfect wind-up to a simple luncheon.

CARAMEL ROLLS

1 cake Fleischmann's Yeast — 9½ cups flour
1 teaspoon sugar — 4 eggs
½ cup lukewarm water — 1 cup sugar
1 cups milk — ¼ teaspoon salt — ½ cup butter

Dissolve the yeast and the sugar in the lukewarm water. Scald the milk and add just enough flour to make a light batter, not a stiff one. Beat well and then let this cool. Add the yeast; again beat well, adding more flour if necessary. Let this rise until light, double its bulk, then add the eggs, sugar, creamed butter, and the salt. Add enough flour so that the dough is just stiff enough to handle. Let the dough rise until it doubles its bulk. Then roll dough half-an-inch thick and fill with the following:

1½ cups sugar — 1 tablespoon cinnamon
1½ cups seeded raisins or currants — ½ cup butter

Mix sugar, raisins or currants and cinnamon and sprinkle over the dough; dot with pieces of butter. Now roll up the dough as for jelly roll and cut off pieces one or one-and-a-half inches thick. Prepare muffin tins as follows: Rub ¾ cup butter and 3 cups brown sugar together to make a paste and mix with 1 cup chopped nuts. Line each tin one-fourth inch or deeper with this mixture. Stand the slices of rolled dough on end in the pan, and bake them about thirty minutes in a moderate oven at 400° F. Be careful not to have the oven too hot, as the sugar in the bottom might burn. Turn out immediately, and keep the sugar side up. Makes 3 dozen.

A stern announcer suggests... The trend away from home baking resumed through the war, when many women took up jobs in defense work. Commercial bakeries continued to grow. Fleischmann's was careful not to compete with commercial baking in its advertising. It was a strange Catch-22 in advertising that circuitously proclaimed, "'Baking day' isn't on the American housewife's calendar any more. For at her bakery or grocery...fresh every day...is a profusion of breads, rolls cakes and pastries that's one of the world's wonders...but there are times when women like to run up a batch of rolls of their own, or try their hand at a coffee cake, just to see if they can still do it!" (A)

When worlds collide. Home baking in the 1950s, although an ideal, was marketed as drudgery that could be relieved by the wizardry of the balloon-hatted baker. By the end of 1946, approximately 85% of all bread consumed in the country was produced by commercial bakers. The remaining 15% were home bakers, composed primarily of rural families, lower income groups, and people of Polish or Scandinavian descent, according to market surveys. Appealing to this market, the company presented "Fast Rising Dry Yeast." The dry yeast product also eliminated the elaborate and costly FedEx-type rapid delivery system with the speeding trucks and dedicated agents. The marketing worked—by 1949 dry yeast accounted for 40% of the market, rising to 69% by 1957. Yet per capita home yeast sales still declined. (A)

Your Baker *now supplies* **a Better Bread for your family!**

Delicious, tender-crusted baker's bread is more important than ever now as the starting point of each meal you plan. For it's been chosen to supply extra B-vitamins and iron to the nation's diet!

The "Enriched" label on your baker's loaf means that it contains additional Thiamine, Niacin, Riboflavin and Iron—important protective factors for all your family!

"Enriched" White Bread is the same as regular white bread in whiteness and lightness, texture and delicious taste. The same in calories—and in our. The same grand source of economical food energy and protein. See your family gets plenty. *It's better for them!*

Enriched with 3 Vitamins and Iron

Published by the makers of Fleischmann's Yeast as a contribution to Canada's national health.

QUICK, THE MIX!

Go ahead and bake-it-easy—that's why mixes were born! And now you can do wonderful new things with them, just by adding Fleischmann's Active Dry Yeast.

COFFEE BREAKERS

¼ cup (½ stick) Fleischmann's Margarine
⅓ cup brown sugar
1 teaspoon light corn syrup
⅓ cup chopped pecans
1 package Fleischmann's Active Dry Yeast
¾ cup very warm water
2½ cups Bisquick
2 tablespoons melted Fleischmann's Margarine
¼ cup brown sugar
1 teaspoon cinnamon

Melt margarine; stir in ⅓ cup brown sugar and syrup, bring to full boil. Spread in large oblong pan. Sprinkle with pecans. Sprinkle yeast into very warm water. Stir to dissolve. Add Bisquick, beat vigorously; turn dough onto board well dusted with Bisquick. Knead until smooth, about 20 times. Roll into 12-inch square. Brush with 2 tablespoons margarine. Combine ¼ cup brown sugar and cinnamon. Sprinkle center third with half the mixture. Fold one-third over center third. Sprinkle with remaining sugar-cinnamon. Fold remaining third over the 2 layers. Cut with sharp knife, crosswise into strips about 1 inch wide. Grasp ends of strip and twist. Seal ends firmly. Place in pan about 1½ inches apart. Cover. Let rise in warm place until doubled in bulk, about 1 hour. Bake at 400°F. about 20 minutes. Invert pan immediately.

By the early 1960s, Fleischmann's had done a back flip by heavily promoting home baking again. American women were developing careers and going off to work—Fleischmann's countered by stating how simple and time-effective it was to bake bread using Fleischmann's yeast. The "Bake it Easy" campaign took the push-button world of the 1950s and applied it to the kitchen, offering "17 recipes grandmother couldn't bake." Those working women who still had pretensions of being good housewives could relieve guilt by using the recipes provided by the test kitchens of Standard Brands. This one offered an easy way of whipping up coffee twists from Fleischmann's margarine and yeast, plus corn syrup, Bisquick, and pecans. (A)

Fleischmann's finally decided to make home baking competitive. It began an education program that promoted the product through 4-H Clubs. Teachers, home economists, and food editors were encouraged to use yeast-leavened products in their classes and publications. The company became active in state fair baking competitions, and over 400,000 4-H girls were involved in yeast-based baking demonstrations. Winners of baking contests were heavily promoted in advertising copy, and recipe books promoted items that could produce award-winning results. Although state fair bake-offs are now an engrained part of Americana, their origin goes back to the empowerment that Charles Fleischmann gave the homemaker in 1868 to produce the finest quality of bread and pastries. (A)

The carefree, domestic chic of the early 1960s reached its prime in the 1963 cookbook. "Gossipy Sweet Buns" was just the order in the days of big hair, purple Capri pants, and Princess® phones. Innovations in yeast production continued along this line with the introduction of RapidMix in 1968 that eliminated the need to dissolve yeast in water. In 1984, research into recombinant DNA in yeast enzymes produced RapidRise Yeast, followed in 1988 with rehydratable Instant Active Dry Yeast. In 1994, the inevitable BreadMachine Yeast hit the shelves.

Nine

FADE AWAYS, MERGERS, AND SPIN-OFFS

In 1976, a young CEO, F. Ross Johnson was appointed as head of Standard Brands. It was said he was driven by the bottom line, not company tradition. He felt that the yeast line was strong but could not grow further. In 1981, the $3 billion Standard Brands merged with the $2.5 billion Nabisco Inc. In 1985, Johnson brokered a deal whereby R.J. Reynolds bought Nabisco Brands for $4.9 billion, with Johnson remaining CEO. In 1986, RJR/Nabisco divested itself of the Fleischmann's Yeast line, selling it to Burns, Philp & Co. of Australia for $130 million. No reason was ever given.

Fleischmann's Yeast then purchased both Dixie Yeast and Anheuser Busch's industrial yeast interests, plus Dromedary line of pimentos, dates, and mixes. In 1988, it purchased Specialty Brands. The amalgamated company was then split into a consumer line and an industrial line, with Specialty Brands marketing Fleischmann Yeast for the home consumer, and Fleischmann's Yeast selling to commercial bakeries.

Burns, Philp of North America is headquartered in Fenton, Missouri, just outside of St. Louis. The highly profitable Fleischmann distilleries had previously been sold to Barton Brands of Chicago, who still produce gin, vodka, rye, blended whiskey, and brandy under the Fleischmann label. Similarly, the Fleischmann's Margarine line that had been introduced at Standard Brands in the 1930s was sold to Beatrice Foods, who subsequently merged with ConAgra.

Burns, Philp continued the long tradition of research to develop new yeast strains. They now harvest yeast with special properties and flavors that are used as food additives and enrichment agents. Fleischmann's still markets directly to the home baker in the familiar yellow packet, having never abandoned the original company's first customers. In 1996, they launched a Website promoting home baking (www.breadworld.com), filled with recipes and tips as true as the first Fleischmann's ad, and still marketed by underwriting baking competitions at fairs and expositions. In 2004, Fleischmann's introduced a program to promote healthy high-fiber recipes.

The commercial production of Fleischmann's yeast was one of the first industrial applications of what is now known as bioengineering. By using pure strains of microbes to produce ethyl alcohol, vinegar, and more yeast, Charles Fleischmann and his family gave America its freshly baked bread, dill pickles, and gin martinis. Yeast was coaxed into producing more vitamin B and D, and was tweaked into producing new flavors and protein additives for the food industry. As the genome of the humble yeast fungus is more thoroughly known, it will continue to lend insight to the greater understanding of basic biological processes, with application to pharmaceutical production in addition to food production. Perhaps in future "Yeast for Health" campaigns the tiny organism will reach its potential as a real miracle food. In the meantime, America's home bakers will continue to be fascinated with the simple magic of turning flour and water into freshly baked bread—something that is truly human.

The Holmes family continued the tradition of innovation and public service brought by both the Fleischmann and Holmes branches. Christian Holmes III (above) served in the Korean War and became a resident of Honolulu for a time, then moved to Texas. He had two sons, Michael and Christian IV. In February 1961, Christian III married actress Arlene Dahl in Reno. Ms. Dahl is the mother of actor Lorenzo Lamas by her previous marriage to Fernando Lamas. Michael, a marine and Vietnam war veteran, is the husband of Ambassador Genta H. Holmes, head of the Foreign Service under Madelene Albright and Clinton's ambassador to Australia; Christian IV served as the number three official at the U.S. Environmental Protection Agency as its Chief Financial Officer. He also directed the U.S. Trade and Development Agency, and received the U.S. Army Soldiers Medal for Heroism. Carl and Jay Holmes stewarded much of the Holmes family holdings from New York in later years, and were heads of the Christian R. Holmes Foundation, established by his mother. Ann Holmes Terrell, daughter of Christian Holmes II and Katherine MacDonald, currently divides her time between Santa Barbara and Reno, as did her great uncle Major Max. She raises avocados and loves tennis.

While in Hawai`i Holmes was known as the "Fleischmann Yeast heir" when being the "Tuna King" might have been more appropriate. Alan Davis in Honolulu managed Christian R. Holmes II Trust and interests in Hawaiian Tuna Packers, which became part of Castle & Cooke. The company now markets its tuna under the Bumble Bee ® label, with scraps becoming Figaro Cat Food ®. The last family member in the yeast business was Gustav Fleischmann II, son of Gustav Sr., and nephew of Charles. He was appointed vice-president of Standard Brands in 1947. He was also the general manager of the company and the Peekskill plant until his retirement in the 1950s. (A)

The famous Coconut Island built by Christian Holmes II lived on. The most private of islands was sold to a group of five prominent businessmen in the late 1940s, the proceeds going to Holmes' three children. After toying with the idea of converting the island into a resort club or commercial hotel, oilman Edwin W. Pauley (right) of Los Angeles began to use the island for a summer home for his family that included three spirited teenagers. Pauley was a powerful fundraiser for the Democratic Party, and used the island to fête many of his political colleagues. He was for years chairman of the Board of Regents for the University of California system. In April of 1953, retiring President Harry S. Truman, wife Bess, and daughter Margaret spent a month relaxing on Coconut Island as Pauley's guest. (TL)

Pauley was good friends and political allies with Governor Edmund "Pat" Brown and his family (his son Jerry Brown, also a governor of California, presidential-hopeful, mayor of Oakland, and the author's current boss, is the boy standing in the center). (PF)

Hawai`i Institute of Marine Biology on Coconut Island was established by Edwin Pauley and Dr. Robert Hiatt, but prefigured by Christian Holmes, who was absorbed in marine biology research as an avocation and as an important Research & Development aspect of his Hawaiian Tuna Packers. Although Christian Holmes II had obtained clear title to Coconut Island, the 16.3 acres of land created by his dredging and filling was apparently never assessed or taxed. Wisely, Pauley turned over control of the filled shoreline to the Territory. In addition, he helped establish a marine biology lab on the island in association with the University of Hawai`i. The Hawai`i Institute of Marine Biology at Coconut Island is now one of the most respected centers for study of corals and other marine life in the world. (HIMB)

The marine center and the ambiance of the spectacular Coconut Island attracted dignitaries from around the world. Here Lady Bird Johnson is escorted by laboratory director Robert Hiatt. (PF)

The popular television sitcom *Gilligan's Island*, starring Bob Denver, Alan Hale Jr., and Jim Backus, is the story of a ship's mate (Gilligan), his skipper, a brainy professor, a movie star, a simple farm girl, and a millionaire and his wife shipwrecked on a small Pacific island. It was Coconut Island in numerous ways: the pilot for the series was filmed in Hawai`i; the lead trailer shows the tour boat leaving Kewalo Basin in Honolulu (location of Honolulu Tuna Packers cannery) and getting caught in a storm; the next scene shows the passengers shipwrecked on beautiful Coconut Island. With its millionaires, movie stars, and professors, art imitated life on Coconut Island. (A)

The real shipwreck on Coconut Island was the schooner Seth Parker, shown here in 1972. At my last visit, it had been reduced to a few long outlines of sawdust in a green lagoon. Most of the Holmes-era buildings are gone now too, except for the private Retreat cottage of Holmes himself. (GN)

Since the 1950s, many other improvements in product and production were put into place. Additives to improve dough for commercial bakers were developed. Yeast strains were perfected to serve as flavor enhancers. At Peekskill, erosterol was extracted from yeast and processed into Vitamin D, further adding to its appeal as an enriched product. Unfortunately, the plant became outdated. In 1979, having produced millions of pounds of yeast, oceans of gin, and lakes of vinegar and margarine, it closed its doors. This is one of the few large buildings remaining of the original site. (A)

However, other production units were located in strategic locations around the county (and several foreign countries), such as this Fleischmann plant outside of Oakland, California. It produced yeast, vinegar, and margarine until its closing in 2002. (A)

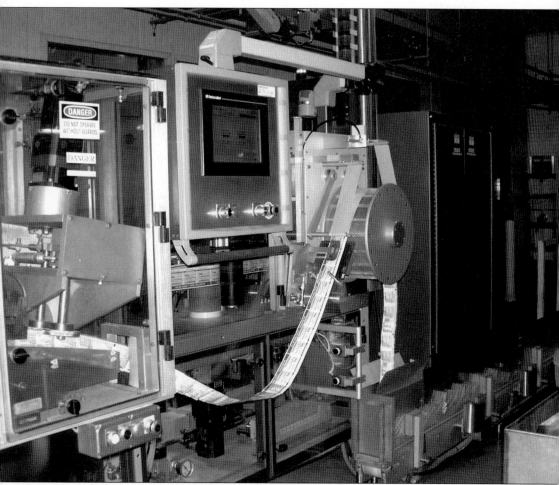

Where rows of women once laboriously wrapped and packaged Fleischmann's Yeast, robots operating in oxygen-free clean rooms now whisk the product through the line. This is the modern packet-sealing station at the LaSalle plant in Québec. (BP)

ACKNOWLEDGEMENTS

This book has had a long and sinuous history. Putting together this chronicle, especially a pictorial one, was daunting. Due to mergers, spin-offs, and family divorces, there was no single rich source of rich corporate and family records. Photographs, letters, tales, artifacts, and anecdotes were scattered to the wind from Hawai`i to Silesia. I had, therefore, to rely on the diligent efforts of scores of family members, archivists, librarians, and former employees to tell me their stories and lend me their photographs.

Having first started this project with a history of Holmes and Pauley's Coconut Island, I thank Dr. Phil Helfrich, Director Emeritus of the Hawai`i Institute of Marine Biology for originally dreaming up the idea and to Dr. Stephen and Marylyn Pauley of the Edwin W. Pauley Foundation of Los Angeles for providing financial support.

Of great inspiration has been the warm friendship of the Fleischmann and Holmes families. I would like to acknowledge Christian Holmes II's daughter Ann Holmes Terrell, her son Bruce Spaulding, and her husband Don; Michael and Ambassador Genta Holmes, and Michael's brother Christian Holmes IV, who has always helped me maintain a clear vision of his grandfather. All have been most generous in sharing information about their family. Thanks also to Charles Fleischmann III of Cincinnati for his particular insight into his family's place in history and his spirited letters.

The Anderson family, Dolores Mokuoloe Beyer Berengue, Col. A.R. Brashear, W. Dudley Childs Jr., Mary Clark, Helen S. Davis, Rose Deang, Bill Drake, Charles Forquer, Steve Gates, Ankita Gouveia, George and Fumiko Harada, Julia Ing, Sen. Dan Inouye, Pamela Larson, Charles Lucas Jr., Richard Miller, Steve Miranda, Harry Myer, Gary Nakamoto, Antonio Pagliotti, Grieg Porter, Samuel Price, Rick Rainalter, Sydney Schwartz, Barbara Shanahan, G.W. Sumner, Doug Uyehara, Ethel Takahashi Uyehara, Henry Walker Jr., Brenda Yette, and Ruth Youngren—I thank for their gracious permission to participate in the gathering of oral histories. My conversations with Paul Breese, first director of the Honolulu Zoo, were very insightful, explaining the extent of Christian Holmes' interest in collecting wild animals. I thank Sherwood Schwartz, creator of *Gilligan's Island*, for his interview.

So much of the work in preparing this book was done not on the white sands of Coconut Island, but in dark and moldy shelves of libraries and archives: I thank Margaret M. Greenan, Ilene P. Karpf, and David R. Stivers of the Fleischmann archives of RJR-Nabisco at Parsippany, New York; Robert Boyle of the Field Library of Peekskill, New York; John Curran of the Peekskill Museum; John Duda of the Skene Memorial Library; Robert Blesse and Kathryn Totten of the Special Collections Department, Library of the University of Nevada—Reno; Special Collections of the University of California—Los Angeles; Sylvia Metzinger of the Public Library of Cincinnati and Hamilton County; executive director Dr. Karl Hutterer and archivist Terri Sheridan of the Santa Barbara Natural History Museum; Linda Bailey and Cynthia Keller of the Cincinnati Museum Center; DeSoto Brown, Betty Kam, Tracy Tam Sing, and Dr. Susan A. Lebo of the Bishop Museum, Honolulu; the University of Hawai`i—Manoa; Hawai`i State Archives; Peggy Tate-Smith of the Mystic Museum; Linda Early of Hillforest Association; Patty Brockman and Carter Randolph of the Green-Acres Foundation, and Billie Broaddus of the University of Cincinnati Medical Heritage Center. I would also like to thank Christine Crawford, Keith Dierburg, James Parker, and Rob Trabert of the Fleischmann Company, and Rabbi Jeffrey Salkin and Geoffrey Reiner of the Community Synagogue at the "Chimneys" at Sands Point. I appreciate all the work and encouragement of Arcadia editor John Pearson, and to Paul Donahue of the California Academy of Sciences.

To Scot Parry I send special appreciation for all his help in the gathering of documents, interviews, and follow-ups to construct this book. To all that have shared their own special encounters with the Fleischmann family and company—thank you!

BIBLIOGRAPHY

BOOKS AND PERIODICALS

Atwan, Robert, Donald McQuade, and John W. Wright. Edsels, Luckies, & Frigidaires. Delta. 1979.

Bergen, Julius. They Helped Make America. University of Nevada Library, Fleischmann collection. Undated ms.

Blum, Daniel. A Pictoral History of the Silent Screen. New York, Grosset & Dunlap. 1953.

Botsford, Gardner. A Life of Privilege, Mostly. New York, St. Martin's Press. 2003.

Cincinnati Chamber of Commerce Papers, The Cincinnati Historical Society, 3:119.

"Coconut Island," Paradise of the Pacific. December 1947.

Devaney, Dennis M., Marion Kelly, Polly Jae Lee, and Lee S. Motteler. Kaneohe: A History of Change. Honolulu, Department of Anthropology, Bishop Museum. 1976.

Fischer, Martin. Christian R. Holmes: Man and Physician. Springfield, IL, Charles C. Thomas. 1937.

Fleischmann, Max. Across the Guaso Nyiro to Mt. Marsabit, 1910. Library of the Santa Barbara Museum of Natural History. Unpublished ms.

Grayson, Melvin. 42 Million a Day: The Story of Nabisco Brands. East Hanover, NJ, Nabisco Brands. 1986.

Hampton, Benjamin. History of the American Film Industry. New York, Dover. 1970.

Kyvig, David. Hard Times, Hopeful Times; Repealing National Prohibition. Chicago, University of Chicago Press. 1979.

Marchand, Roland. Advertising the American Dream. Berkeley, University of California Press. 1985.

"Medicine and Madison Avenue, United States of America vs. The Fleischmann Company, Docket #1989." Printer's Ink, 184(5):53. August 4, 1938.

New Yorker Records 1924-1984. Center for the Humanities, New York Public Library.

O'Brien, Eileen. "The Saga of Chris Holmes," Paradise of the Pacific, 56. Honolulu, May 1944.

Pulfer, Laura. "A Last, Guilty, Wistful Look at Old Money," The Cincinnati Enquirer, May 7, 1996. http://www.enquirer.com/columns/pulfer/1996/05/050796_lp.html.

Randall, Monica. The Mansions of Long Island's Gold Coast. Rizzoli. 1979.

Reports of the Board of Commissioners, Cincinnati Industrial Exposition 1872, 1873. Cincinnati, Order of the Board.

Roe, George Mortimer, Hon. Julius Fleischmann. Cincinnati, The Queen City, Volume 3. Cincinnati, Cincinnati Post-Star Company. 1905(?).

Rolker, A.W. "Louis Fleischmann and his Bread Line," Pearson's Magazine. December 1904.

Rumsey, L.A. "Progress of Education in Baking," Baking Industry, April 12, 1952. J. Walter Thompson Company Archives.

Sharps, Victoria. Letter to Charles Fleischmann III, October 31, 2000. Author's collection.

Standard Brands Inc. Annual Report. 1929.

Thomas, Louis R. and H. Lew Wallace. "Stokowski on Podium," Queen City Heritage. Summer 1984.

Wright, Steven L. 125 Years and Still Rising: History of the Fleischmann Company, 1868-1993. 1993.

WEBSITES

Federal Trade Commission complaint against The Fleischmann Company. http://scriptorium.lib.duke.edu:80/mma/ad-images/MM11/MM1160-0172dpi.html

Fleischmanns, NY Museum of Memories. http://www.catskill.net/fleisch/museum.htm

German Beer History. http://www.oldworld.ws/okbeerhist.html

New Exhibit Celebrates Jewish Kitchen. http://www.cincypost.com/living/1999/kitch091499.html

Remembrances of Eleuthera by Gertrude Moller. www.jaxshells.org/remb.htm

Roasted Peacocks And Performing Ducks. http://www.naples.net/history/naples/roasted.htm

Seth Parker, The Offshore Radio Fleet. http://www.offshore-radio.de/fleet/sethparker.htm

What are yeasts? http://www.yeastgenome.org/VL-what_are_yeast.html

yeast, science, & history. http://www.cofalec.com/sciee.htm

(C)